GLOBETROTTER™

Travel

GW00634445

COPENHAGEN AND DENMARK

RICHARD SALE

NEW
HOLLAND

NEW
HOLLAND

| ★★★ Highly recommended |
| ★★ Recommended |
| ★ See if you can |

Second edition published in 2007
by New Holland Publishers (UK) Ltd
London • Cape Town • Sydney • Auckland
10 9 8 7 6 5 4 3 2 1

website: www.newhollandpublishers.com

Garfield House, 86 Edgware Road
London W2 2EA, United Kingdom

80 McKenzie Street
Cape Town 8001, South Africa

14 Aquatic Drive, Frenchs Forest
NSW 2086, Australia

218 Lake Road, Northcote
Auckland, New Zealand

Distributed in the USA by
The Globe Pequot Press, Connecticut

ISBN 978 1 84537 634 5

Keep us Current
Information in travel guides is apt to change, which is
why we regularly update our guides. We'd be grateful
to receive feedback if you've noted something we
should include in our updates. If you have new information, please share it with us by writing to the
Publishing Manager, Globetrotter, at the office near-
est to you (addresses on this page). The most signifi-
cant contribution to each new edition will receive a
free copy of the updated guide.

Publishing Manager: Thea Grobbelaar
DTP Cartographic Manager: Genené Hart
Editors: Nicky Steenkamp, Thea Grobbelaar
Design and DTP: Nicole Bannister, Lellyn Creamer
Cartographers: Marisa Roman, Nicole Bannister
Picture Researcher: Shavonne Govender
Consultant: Hugh Taylor

Reproduction by Hirt & Carter (Pty) Ltd, Cape Town
Printed and bound by Times Offset (M) Sdn. Bhd.,
Malaysia

Photographic Credits:
FAN Photo Agency/jonarnoldimages.com: page 86;
Photo Access: title page, page 29;
Richard Sale: cover, pages 7, 8, 12, 17, 18, 19, 20,
22, 25, 26, 27, 30, 33, 35, 37, 38, 40, 41, 42, 44, 45,
46, 47, 49, 50, 51, 52, 55, 60, 63, 64, 65, 66, 68, 69,
70, 72, 73, 74, 76, 81, 83, 84, 88, 90, 91, 93, 94, 95,
96, 98, 102, 103, 104, 106, 107, 109, 110, 111;
Richard Sale Collection: page 105;
Neil Setchfield: pages 4, 21, 23, 34, 36, 56, 57, 82;
Jeroen Snijders: pages 6, 9, 11, 14, 15, 16, 39, 53,
80, 108, 114;
The Seeing Eye/ Anders Blomqvist: pages 116, 119;
Travel Ink/Stephen Coyne: page 120;
Travel Ink/Patrick Ford: page 28.

Although every effort has been made to ensure that
this guide is up to date and current at time of going
to print, the Publisher accepts no responsibility or lia-
bility for any loss, injury or inconvenience incurred
by readers or travellers using this guide.

Cover: *Tourists create a lively atmosphere in the
squares of Denmark.*
Title page: *The famous Little Mermaid, Copenhagen.*

CONTENTS

1. **Introducing Copenhagen and Denmark** **4**
   The Land 6
   History in Brief 12
   Government and Economy 24
   The People 25

2. **Copenhagen** **30**
   Rådhuspladsen 33
   Around Tivoli 35
   Strøget 38
   Slotsholmen 41
   Nyhavn 44
   Frederiksstaden 46
   Rosenborg 52
   Christianshavn 54
   Vesterbro 56

3. **North Jutland** **60**
   Aalborg 62
   The Very North 64
   Limfjorden 65
   Himmerland and Central Jutland 67
   Århus 70
   Silkeborg and the Lakes 73

4. **South Jutland** **76**
   Jelling and Billund 77
   Esbjerg 80
   Ribe 81
   The Far South 82

5. **Fyn** **86**
   Odense 88
   West Fyn 91
   South Fyn 93
   The Fyn Islands 94
   Nyborg and East Fyn 95

6. **Zealand** **98**
   West Zealand 100
   Roskilde 102
   Northeast Zealand 104
   South Zealand 110
   Lolland, Falster and Møn 112

7. **Bornholm** **116**
   Rønne and a Tour of Bornholm 118

Travel Tips **122**

Index **127**

1. Introducing Copenhagen and Denmark

Denmark has a habit of confounding the expectations of visitors. Those remembering tales of murderous Viking raids are surprised to find a country of friendly, helpful, gentle people. Visitors recalling that this is Scandinavia will be surprised at how different it is to Norway and Sweden. Those wondering what to expect from a country which abolished censorship decades ago are sure to be disappointed by a well-adjusted country with people who, despite the lurid suggestions of some, do not have an obsession with dodgy images.

There are Viking remains, some of the finest that survive anywhere – the rune stones at Jelling, the Viking ships at Roskilde – but Denmark is also the country of Hans Christian Andersen. Some of his tales have a darker side, it is true, but a nation whose best-loved writer produced stories for children has clearly left its past well behind.

The Danes share a common ancestry with their Scandinavian cousins, but they are a more relaxed people, the absence of a harsh, rugged land rubbing the harder edges off their character. Those who look hard will find the more liberal material that follows from a lack of censorship, but as it has been pointed out often, it is chiefly where the visitors, not the Danes, are to be found.

For so small a country – Jutland perched on top of Germany and a collection of islands in the Baltic Sea – Denmark has so much more to offer than the stereotypes. Looking beyond the Little Mermaid the visitor will find a vibrant country, with history, art and scenery to amaze, where style and substance combine. A marvellous place.

TOP ATTRACTIONS

*** Jelling: Viking rune stones.
*** Odense: a beautiful city.
*** Tivoli: Copenhagen's fun park.
** Ribe: Denmark's oldest town.
** Legoland: children's paradise.
** Roskilde: Viking ships.
* Den Gamle By: Denmark's best open-air museum, located at Århus.
* National Museum, Copenhagen: a stunning collection.
* Egeskov: something for everyone here.

Opposite: *Hans Christian Andersen gazes towards Tivoli in this fine sculpture.*

Above: *In northern Jutland sand driven by North Sea winds threatens to overwhelm coastal villages.*

THE LAND

Since no point in Denmark is more than 52km (32 miles) from the sea, and since the highest point fails to reach the 180m (591ft) contour, it might be imagined that the Danish countryside was flat and dull, geography not having a chance to get going before the sea arrived again to cut it short. This view is reinforced when, on an internal flight, the country below appears to be little more than an ordered array of fields. In part this is a true reflection of the country, Denmark being one of the most intensively cultivated and altered landscapes in Europe. But at the same time it is an oversimplification.

It is claimed that by the end of the 19th century less than 5% of Denmark's original woodland areas remained intact and that most of the heath and moorland had been claimed for agriculture, just as much of the coastal marginal land had been turned into arable farmland by draining the salt marshes. The Common Agricultural Policy of the European Union is now accused of adding to the exploitation of the Danish countryside, making it one of the most intensively altered landscapes in Europe. Thankfully a growing environmental awareness, and the alteration of agricultural subsidies which makes the farming of some land less viable, means that the situation is being reversed. Inevitably the reversal will be slow and the aspirations of the environmentalists must be limited by the realities of the situation, but it is planned to double the acreage of woodland by the end of the present century and to restore large tracts of salt marshes.

The Coast

With around 7250km (about 4500 miles) of coastline it would seem that Denmark is an ideal country to display the full range of coastal scenery. But the limited geological diversity of the country and its general flatness means that only a small portion of that scenic range is present. Not that such a limitation should be taken as indicating that

Denmark has little to offer. It has wonderful coastal scenery with a couple of quite surprising features.

The main features of the Danish coast are the **beaches** and the **dunes** in both of which the country can compete with the very best. Almost the entire western coast of Jutland is beach, attracting Germans by the thousands, many of them owning holiday homes in the area, and many more using the large number of well-appointed camp sites. The island of **Rømø**, lying close to the German border, is very popular, though the sea retreats a long way from the most spectacular beach at Lakolk on the west coast.

Further to the north, **Fanø** – Rømø and Fanø are Denmark's two North Sea islands – has a nudist beach. There is a string of popular beaches to the northeast of Esbjerg – between **Blåvand** and **Henne Strand** – to the north of which lies **Holmsland Klit**. This extraordinary sand bar, 35km (22 miles) long and often barely 1km (about 0.5 miles) wide, separates the North Sea from **Ringkøbing Fjord**. Both the sea and the fjord are excellent for windsurfers, while the dunes that surmount the bar are a joy. For the bather the sea must be treated with caution: Denmark's North Sea coast is not suitable for the novice swimmer and children especially should be carefully supervised.

The beaches of **Jammerbugten** in north Jutland tend to be safer (**Lønstrup** is particularly good), but here too caution is needed. Winds sweeping across the North Sea often pile up water onto Jutland's coast in spectacular fashion, but the spectacle can be a danger to the unwary. The same wind also creates the dunes which back the beaches, those around **Råbjerg Mile** and **Skagen** being among the largest and most attractive in the country.

Set among these strips of beach and dune are areas of different scenery. At several spots there are salt marshes and mud flats, places where the distinction between land and sea has become blurred. Of these the best are at **Højer** and

ISLANDS GALORE

Denmark comprises 406 islands about 100 of which are inhabited. The largest island is Zealand (Sjælland) – on which Copenhagen stands – followed by Fyn, Lolland and Falster (to the south of Zealand) and Bornholm. The Jutland border with Germany, the only connection with mainland Europe, is 69km (42 miles) long. That compares with a coastline of some 7250km (around 4500 miles). Nowhere in Denmark is more than 52km (32 miles) from the sea. The island of Bornholm, in the Baltic Sea to the east of Zealand, actually lies closer to Sweden and Poland than it does to any other part of Denmark.

Below: *On Jutland's western coast the beaches are beautiful, though sometimes lashed by the turbulent North Sea.*

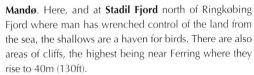

Mandø. Here, and at **Stadil Fjord** north of Ringkøbing Fjord where man has wrenched control of the land from the sea, the shallows are a haven for birds. There are also areas of cliffs, the highest being near Ferring where they rise to 40m (130ft).

On Jutland's eastern, Baltic, shore, the scenery is more varied. There are still fine beaches, **Als**, an island off the southeast Jutland shore, being a popular resort crowded with camp sites and holiday lets. But there are also sheltered coves and deeply indented fjords – **Mariager Fjord**, **Randers Fjord**, and the **Haderslev Fjord** are Denmark's narrowest. Though not approaching the grandeur of Norway's fjords, the Jutland inlets do offer occasional delightful views.

Fyn's coastline is mainly beach and dune, much of it very popular with holiday-makers. Of the holiday areas the most popular are the **southeast coast**, between Nyborg and Svendborg, and the whole of the island of **Langeland**. Langeland's beaches, being very safe, are par-ticularly suitable for children. On the north coast of Fyn, **Hindsholm** with its 25m (82ft) cliffs and the marvellous beaches and dune-scapes of **Flyvesand Point** and the **Agernæs Peninsula** stand out.

Zealand also has fine beaches. That below the Louisiana art gallery at **Humlebæk** is delightful, but by common consent the best is at **Hornbæk**, with that at **Dronningmølle** coming a close second. In reality that compe-tition has too few entries, since many of the villages of north Zealand have beaches of soft white sand backed by rose-topped dunes.

Beaches are to be found all along Zealand's coasts and those of **Lolland** and **Falster** to the south, with two very notable exceptions. At **Stevns Klint**, at the southeast-ern tip of Zealand, and at **Møns Klint**, at the eastern tip of Møn, there are spectacular chalk cliffs. At **Højerup** the crumbling chalk has undermined the church, adding a story of natural disaster to the beauty of the coast.

Only on **Bornholm**, Denmark's extreme easterly island, does the coastal scenery change dramatically. There, at the northern end of the island, hard, angular granite produces a landscape closer to that of Norway's fjords than Denmark's softer, flatter edges.

Inland

Drives through inland Denmark pass through wonderful pastoral scenery, the view of it often made easier by the lack of obscuring roadside hedges. Whenever a small rise occurs there is an expansive view of a patchwork of fields dotted with clumps of trees. But excellent though these views are, as noted earlier the landscape seen is one almost entirely transformed from the natural. One survey has even suggested that less than 5% of the courses of Denmark's streams and rivers remain unaltered by man.

Yet there are patches of undisturbed country, roads in central Jutland occasionally passing areas of heathland. Altogether about 5% of Denmark's area is now designated as conservation area land, this including not only heath, but some remnant moorland, woodland (including coastal forests) and lakes. Of these areas the best known is the forest of **Rold Skov**, the centrepiece of **Rebild Bakker** – Denmark's only national park. To the east of the park, towards the coast of Aalborg Bay, **Lille Vildmose** (Little Moor) is the remnant of an ancient area of moorland, while to the southeast the rounded peninsula of **Djursland** is a fine mix of moor and wood, with some good beaches at the peninsula's edge.

South of Rebild Bakker, **Silkeborg** is the centre of another area of beautiful natural scenery. This area is occasionally referred to as Denmark's Lake District but comprises not only lakes, but the country's highest peaks and a section of the longest river. The scenery is pastoral rather than dramatic, and on a human rather than a grand scale, but is nonetheless very pretty.

Above: *The Danish landscape is one of the most altered in Europe, but still offers lovely pastoral views.*
Opposite: *The Danes are great cyclists. Here a lone cyclist contends with sand heaped on the road by North Sea winds.*

A FOOT IN EACH SEA

Beyond Skagen lies Grenen, a spit of sand which can be reached by a half-hour walk from the road's end. Denmark's most northerly point lies along the curve of dunes here, but the chief reason for taking the walk – apart from the sheer beauty of the area – is the rush of water at the tip. To the left is the North Sea, to the right the Baltic Sea, the thrash of water being the point at which the two meet. The intrepid can place a foot in either sea, but please note that swimming is not allowed, the ripping tides having carried off many unsuspecting bathers.

COPENHAGEN	J	F	M	A	M	J	J	A	S	O	N	D
MAX TEMP. °C	2	2	5	10	16	19	22	21	18	12	7	4
MIN TEMP. °C	-2	-3	-1	4	8	11	14	14	11	7	3	1
MAX TEMP. °F	36	36	41	50	61	66	72	70	64	54	45	34
MIN TEMP. °F	28	27	30	39	46	52	57	57	52	45	37	32
HOURS OF SUN DAILY	1	2	4	5	8	8	8	7	5	3	1	1
RAINFALL mm	49	39	32	38	40	47	71	66	62	59	48	49
RAINFALL in.	1.9	1.5	1.3	1.5	1.6	1.9	2.8	2.6	2.4	2.3	1.9	1.9
DAYS OF RAINFALL	17	13	12	13	11	13	14	14	15	16	16	17

Opposite: *Areas of real wilderness are rare in Denmark, but there are still places where wild flowers bloom.*

A well-signposted walking path of about 65km (40 miles) links Silkeborg with **Skanderborg**, taking in many of the best sites the area has to offer.

Fyn and Zealand have little to compare with Jutland, though on Zealand there is lovely country – woods and lakes – to the east of Slagelse.

Climate

Copenhagen lies at about the same latitude as Moscow and Ketchikan (in southern Alaska), but the **Gulf Stream**, the warm Atlantic current that washes the shores of northern Europe, takes the edge off the extremes of temperature experienced by these two, and other places that lie equally far north. In winter, though temperatures do fall to, and below, 0°C (32°F), it is very rare for them to even approach the legendary colds of the Moscow winter. While the temperate climate the Gulf Steam bestows is a blessing in easing winter's chills, the warm air above it is laden with moisture so that Denmark is often cloudy and rain falls during all months of the year. Indeed, the variation in rainfall between the months is remarkably small, the driest month seeing half the rain of the wettest. Despite this, and the relative narrowness of Denmark from east to west, there are noticeable differences in rainfall, Fyn being wetter than Zealand, and Jutland an average of the two.

Flora and Fauna

What little remains of Denmark's original forest comprises deciduous trees, oak and beech dominating the species list. In Denmark, as in other European countries, the population of elm trees has been savagely hit by Dutch elm disease. Most of the commercial forests which have been planted are conifer, though – as noted above – there is now a concerted effort to re-establish woodland with the original mix of tree types.

Many of the dune systems have been planted with **marram** and **lyme grass** in order to stabilize them. The dunes have also been colonized by ***Rosa rugosa***, a non-native species which occasionally grows vigorously, blooming with a profusion of white and pink flowers. To these bursts of colour are added the delicate blush of **thrift** (or sea pink as it is occasionally known).

The bogs and marshlands support many different species of sedges and marshes, as well as typical bog flowers, and the southern coastline also supports the **fleabane** *Inula brittanica*. Another member of the daisy family has a special place in Denmark, the **marguerite** (ox-eye daisy) being the national flower. As Denmark still has strong links with Greenland it is perhaps appropriate that the Greenlandic national flower, **rosebay willowherb**, also grows in abundance.

Intensive farming has reduced the population of many Danish **mammals** and only lucky visitors or those with a particular interest are likely to see many. Red, roe and fallow deer are all present, as are many of Europe's smaller mammals. The otter is an example of the success of recent conservation efforts, the population having increased substantially over the last few years. On Æbelø, off Fyn's northern coast, mouflon (a small wild sheep, a native of Corsica and Sardinia) were introduced in the 1950s. The island is a conservation area, with concerns over the effect of a herd of 100 fallow deer on tree regeneration, and the status of the mouflon is to be considered in the light of this.

The intensive farming that has reduced the number of Danish mammals has also reduced the habitats of many **birds** that were formerly common. On the positive

RARE TERNS

The gull-billed tern is one of the rarest of European terns, its population officially classified as 'vulnerable' and confined to the northern shores of the Mediterranean and Black seas. Apart, that is, from a small population that nests on Fjandø, an island in Nissum Fjord on Jutland's west coast, a remnant group, perhaps from when the Baltic climate was warmer. As well as these very rare birds, Denmark is also a breeding site for two other rare species of tern – the Caspian tern and the black tern.

TOADS AND FROGS

Despite its northerly latitude Denmark is home to no fewer than 11 species of frogs and toads. As well as the common frog there are moor, agile, pool and edible frogs and the common tree frog. The bright green tree frog is the focus of a special conservation program on Bornholm because its population has shrunk by 90% over the last half century. Denmark's toads are the common, spadefoot, natterjack, green and fire-bellied. The green toad is a mottled green and cream, the most attractive amphibian viewed from above, but when the toads are turned over, the fire-bellied wins all competitions for toad attractiveness, its underside being splotched with red and black.

Below: *A dolmen near Lindeskov, one of Denmark's foremost Stone-Age sites.*

side, the number of salt marshes and mud flats, and the decision to increase that number, means that wader and water-bird numbers are stable or increasing. **Black-tailed godwit**, **ruff**, **avocet** and **eider duck** are relatively common, while **marsh harriers** and **honey buzzards** are among the more unusual raptors. Denmark is on the migration route of species travelling south from Norway and Sweden, a fact which brings many bird-watchers to the country. A spectacle which also attracts bird-watchers is the 'Black Sun' of southwest Jutland, when vast flocks of starlings fly in to roost.

HISTORY IN BRIEF

Though conclusive evidence is lacking (or, at least, subject to debate), it is likely that Denmark was settled by hunter-gatherers following the ice north during the interglacial periods of the last Ice Age. These nomadic folk might have explored the country as long ago as 80,000BC, though that date is highly speculative, most experts going no further than 'more than 20,000 years ago'.

The Stone Age

The first permanent settlers arrived in about 10,000BC when the ice finally retreated for good. The ice left an Arctic-like tundra over which reindeer roamed, attracting the nomadic hunters who were the first Danes. As the climate improved the reindeer moved north, and forests replaced the low tundra shrub. At first the earliest Danes, lacking their major prey, would have migrated to the coast to feed on fish and shellfish, but as agriculture replaced hunting and gathering permanent settlements would have arisen in clearings in the forest created by slash-and-burn methods. Around 3500BC man left his first permanent mark on the landscape, erecting tombs to house the dead. These tombs comprised huge flat slabs of stone, several upright and one forming a roof, these stone boxes being earthed over to form **long burrows**. In many cases the earth of the burrow has now blown away leaving the stone boxes – **dolmens** – as gaunt and enigmatic reminders of the past. The tombs imply ritual burial and, therefore, a belief system, but nothing can be said about the beliefs of those Stone-Age Danes, and little more can be inferred about their society.

The Bronze Age

Some time around 1500BC bronze found its way to Denmark, the metal being used not only to fashion tools and weapons, but also jewellery and other works of art.

LURS

Lurs are strangely curved musical instruments dating from the Bronze Age. They feature in the famous 1914 Viking statue by Anton Rosen atop a pillar in Copenhagen's Town Hall Square. The statue is much loved by city folk who claim that the lurs actually sound each time a virgin passes the pillar.

HISTORICAL CALENDAR

ca. 3500BC Man makes his first mark on the Danish landscape.

ca. 1500BC Bronze Age produces beautiful objects.

500BC Angles inhabit southern Jutland.

AD500 First Vikings arrive in Denmark.

793 The Viking Age begins. Danes trade with and plunder northern Europe and Russia.

826 Ansgar arrives to convert the Danes.

ca. 950 Gorm the Old conquers most of Denmark.

ca. 950 Gorm's son Harald Bluetooth unifies Denmark and Norway, makes Christianity the official religion.

1018 Knud (Canute) becomes king of Denmark, England, Norway and southern Sweden.

ca. 1035 Knud dies, Danish empire collapses.

1086 Knud the Holy is murdered.

1157 Valdemar I unifies country after years of internal strife.

1397 The Kalmar Union unites Denmark, Norway and Sweden. King Erik makes Copenhagen his capital.

1523 Kalmar Union dissolved.

1534 Danish Lutheran Church established.

1658 Treaty of Roskilde. Denmark loses last Swedish holdings.

1660 Bornholm revolts and returns to Danish crown.

1721 Hans Egede visits Greenland, establishing the Danish claim.

1772 Struensee executed.

1801 British fleet destroys Danish fleet.

1807 British fleet bombards Copenhagen.

1814 Denmark loses Norway, but keeps Iceland, Faroes and Greenland

1843 Tivoli Gardens opened.

1864 Danes defeated at Dybbøl, lose Schleswig-Holstein.

1914–18 Denmark remains neutral during War.

1920 Plebiscite agrees Jutland border between Denmark and Germany.

1924 Social Democrats gain power.

1940 Germany occupies Denmark but allows Danish autonomy.

1943 Danish government resigns. Germany imposes rule. Denmark joins Allies.

1945 Denmark liberated by the Allies.

1972 Queen Margrethe II is crowned. Denmark joins forerunner of European Union.

1986 Danes vote narrowly for closer links with Europe.

1992–93 Danes vote against, then for Maastricht Treaty.

1996 Copenhagen named European City of Culture.

1998 Danes do not enter Eurozone.

1998 Great Belt Bridge completed.

2000 Bridge between Denmark and Sweden over Øresund completed.

2002 Metro line opens in Copenhagen.

2004 Crown prince Frederick marries the Australian Mary Donaldson.

2005 Bicentennary of birth of Hans Christian Andersen.

One of the finest pieces, a **sun chariot**, and several **lurs** can be seen in the National Museum in Copenhagen. The sun chariot was unearthed in 1902 by a Zealand farmer: it is believed to date from about 1200BC and is exquisitely beautiful – a gilded horse pulling a chariot on which sits a gilded sun disc.

Above: *This sun chariot is one of the finest pieces of Bronze-Age art found in Denmark. It is now in the National Museum.*
Opposite: *With his full beard and animal horn drinking vessel, this Dane is maintaining the Viking tradition.*

Bronze-Age Danes traded with places as far away as Greece: there is no tin in Denmark, and the amber which is found all along Jutland's North Sea coast was used to barter for it. They buried their dead beneath mounds which still adorn today's landscape. That at **Borum**, to the east of Århus, covered the bodies of a man, a woman and a young man, each in a coffin formed by splitting an oak trunk lengthwise.

The Iron Age

In about 500BC iron replaced bronze as the metal of choice for tools and weapons. The iron arrived in Denmark with people now gathered under the general heading of Celts who originated in central Europe and migrated to colonize almost the whole of the habitable north. The use of iron ploughs allowed fields to be cultivated with much greater efficiency, and large agriculture-based communities developed. But despite this settled agrarian existence, these were dangerous times. The Romans noted the enthusiasm the Celts had for intertribal warfare, a fact which they, and later invaders, were quick to exploit. As noted by Tacitus, it was the Celtic Anglii (the Angles) tribe that inhabited southern Jutland, and some of their number joined the Saxons and Jutes who invaded southern Britain to fill the power vacuum after the Romans departed. It was the Angles who gave their name to England.

The dangers of the times were not confined to warfare. Throughout northern Europe around 1500 bog

---

AT HOME IN THE IRON AGE

The Iron-Age Danes lived in long – up to 20m (66ft) – rectangular houses that were orientated east-west, the axis of the rising and setting sun. The houses had thatched roofs held aloft by thick wooden poles, the spaces between the poles filled in with wattle and daub. In each house the people lived at one end, sleeping on platforms around the walls and with a central fire, while their animals occupied the other end. Excavations show that single houses existed, but usually many were grouped together to form a village.

bodies have been found, about 600 of these in Denmark, though many have been lost since peat cutters have been discovering them since medieval times. Of these bodies the best known and preserved are **Tollund Man** and **Grauballe Man**, both found in Jutland. **Elling Woman**, found in Bjældskoval (near Bøllingsø and close to Tollund Man), is another well-preserved bog body. These bodies date from the Romano-Celtic period. Indeed, all three may have been contemporaries, and also contemporaries of Julius Caesar; carbon dating places their deaths at around 60BC ±150 years. Though Grauballe Man had been killed by a blow to the head, the Bjældskoval pair had died by hanging, the man's body showing signs of gentle aftercare which implied a ritual killing rather than an execution.

The Vikings

It is believed that around AD500 a tribe migrated south from Scandinavia to colonize the islands of Denmark, occupying the homeland of the Anglii. These were the Danes, and the present-day language of the country is traceable to these migrants. The Danes were farmers, much like the people they found there when they arrived, but they were also seafarers. The long-boats that were to terrorize half of Europe developed from the craft that brought the settlers across the tricky waters of the Kattegat and Skagerrak. The Danes and the Norsemen of Scandinavia who brought havoc in their longboats are now collectively referred to as the Vikings.

The **Viking Age** is usually said to have begun with the raid in June 793 on the monastery of Lindisfarne on England's northeast coast. The rich, but poorly defended churches and monasteries of Britain were easy targets, but Vikings ranged much further afield.

Why did the Bog People Die?

The Roman writer Tacitus, in his book *Germanic*, a description of northern Europe, noted that the Anglii who inhabited southern Jutland worshipped an earth-mother goddess called Nerthus. At special ceremonies, he says, ornate carts were provided for the goddess to use to tour her realm. After the ceremony the carts were washed in sacred lakes, the slaves who carried out this ritual cleansing then being drowned in the lake. Beautifully decorated carts have indeed been found in some bogs and though the bog people are not definitely thought to have been part of this ceremony, presumably they were sacrificed to appease the gods.

VIKING = PIRATE?

In Old Norse the word *vik* means a cove or bay, a place where a ship could be safely moored. But it seems likely that *viking* meant a pirate raid, those who carried out such raids being *vikingr*, pirates, so perhaps the Vikings also raided their own kind, mooring their longboats in sheltered bays before moving inland to pillage. Although Viking is now employed as a general term for Scandinavians of the period, the Swedes, Norse (or Norwegians) and Danes were separate peoples, though clearly linked by language, religion and culture.

They raided French monasteries and towns. A Frankish monk writing at Noirmoutier, an island off Brittany's extreme southern coast, in the 860s notes 'The number of ships grows: the endless stream of Vikings knows no end. Everywhere Christians are victims of massacres, fire, plunderings: the Vikings overwhelm all in their path and no one can stand against them.' The writer goes on to note that 'Bordeaux, Toulouse, Tours, Orleans have been destroyed, Rouen laid waste, Paris captured, Chartres captured and Bayeux plundered'. The monk runs out of verbs of annihilation long before he runs out of towns.

The Vikings also ranged much further than France and England, raiding Lisbon, Cadiz and Seville, towns on Africa's Mediterranean coast, and reaching Italy where they pillaged Pisa. Crossing the Atlantic they settled Iceland and Greenland, and eventually reached the coast of North America.

But despite the raiding and the voyages of exploration, most Vikings stayed at home, farming the land and developing a thriving trade in agricultural produce and crafts. The farmers lived in small villages. Each farmstead was a long timber building which the family shared with 20 or so head of cattle – people at one end, cows at the other and a fire between the two. There would also be other wooden buildings in the village – barns and workshops. When the trading of farm surpluses made landowners rich, their wooden buildings grew in size, some reaching 50m (165ft) in length. In such vast 'palaces' animals were excluded, and purpose-built cowsheds and stables housed the stock.

Trade with neighbouring countries was carried on through ports serviced by ships that were longer, broader versions of the piratical longboat. The Viking Ship Museum at **Roskilde** (*see page 102*) includes cargo vessels as

Below: *An accurate reproduction of a long-house at the Viking site of Trelleborg on Zealand.*

well as the feared war-
ships. The oldest town in
Denmark, **Ribe**, began as a
trading port. Indeed, Ribe
seems to have owed its
existence entirely to trade,
having been founded in
about 700 and rapidly
becoming the hub for
trade between the peoples
of western Europe and
those of Scandinavia and

the Baltic. Equally important was **Hedeby**, a town in
Schleswig-Holstein, then Danish but now part of
Germany. Set at the border of the Frankish empire with
the Viking lands, Hedeby was later to become larger
than Ribe, though today only the remains of its ramparts
can be seen.

Above: *The town of Ribe,
the oldest in the country,
as seen from the top of
the cathedral.*

Hedeby's ramparts indicate that despite the successes
of commerce, there was an undercurrent of suspicion
and hostility between Denmark and its neighbours – not
surprising when viewed against the background of
Viking raids. Added to the resentments of piracy and the
cultural differences there was also a difference in belief.
The Danes worshipped the pagan pantheon of Viking
gods, though there was no unified system of belief; different regions of Viking Scandinavia pledged allegiance
to different groups of gods. These differences probably
explain differing burial customs. In Denmark only one
ship burial has been discovered – at Ladby – though
many of the graves at Lindholm Høje are surrounded by
stones placed in the shape of a longboat.

In the 9th century Danish paganism became a target
for the Christian Franks. **Ansgar**, a Benedictine monk,
crossed the border in 826 and built the first church in
Ribe, but the conversion of the country took another
150 years. The change from paganism to Christianity
corresponds with the emergence of Denmark as a unified nation. In about 950 *Gorm den Gamle*, **Gorm the
Old**, established Jelling, in Jutland, and the centre of

NAME THAT DAY

The Danish influence on
England (and, consequently,
the English-speaking world)
can be seen in the days of
the week, several of which
are named for the Viking
pantheon. The supreme
god was Odin, or Wodin, for
whom Wednesday is named.
Odin was married to Frigga
who named Friday. Their son
was Thor, god of thunder
(but also of agriculture).
Thursday is named for him,
while Tuesday is named for
Tyr, or Tow, the god of war.

SVEIN FORKBEARD

Though he conquered England, Svein's reign was one of the shortest of any English king. He assumed control on Christmas Day 1013, but died on 2 (or 3) February 1014 after he fell from his horse. Svein was in his mid-forties and, it is conjectured, was exhausted from campaigning.

CANUTE AND THE SEA

Svein Forkbeard's son Knud has become famous as King Canute, the English king who attempted to hold back the sea. This perhaps apocryphal tale is widely misunderstood. It is usually told as the story of an arrogant king ordering the tide not to come in to prove that even the sea obeyed his command. In reality Canute was showing his courtiers that their view of him was wrong, that he was not all powerful and could not stem the flow of the tide.

power in Denmark. Gorm is now seen as the first Danish king and the present royal family can trace their lineage from him, making Denmark the oldest kingdom in Europe. However, as the larger rune stone at **Jelling** notes, it was Gorm's son, **Harald Bluetooth**, who unified the country and, at the same time, established Christianity as the state religion. Denmark's four Viking ring fortresses – two of which, **Fyrkat** (see page 68) and **Trelleborg** (see page 100), have been thoroughly researched – date from this time. Under Harald's successor, **Svein Forkbeard**, Denmark invaded England, forcing Aethelred the Unready to flee and creating an Anglo-Danish kingdom. On Svein's death his eldest son, Harald II, became king of Denmark, and his younger son Knud (more commonly written 'Canute' in English) took the English Crown. In 1018 Harald died and Canute became king of England, Norway and southern Sweden. Canute's empire did not long survive his death. Though there were short-lived reigns by his two sons, by 1042, seven years after Canute's death, the Saxon Edward the Confessor was England's king. In the wake of the Norman conquest of 1066 Danish kings attempted to re-establish control of England, but were met by ruthless Norman resistance: after only 50 years the Anglo-Danish kingdom was no more.

An Age of Unrest

Following the collapse of Canute's northern empire the Kingdom of Denmark, which included Norway (as least, as far as the Arctic Circle) and southern Sweden, was riven by internal strife. At first this was due to conflict between the Bishop of Hamburg, the leader of the Danish church and therefore a man of great influence, and the king.

Canute II, more properly called Knud II, who came to the throne in 1080, attempted to move the state and the Danish church closer together. For his good work he was known as **Knud the Holy**, but his piety did not extend to his subjects. He introduced Denmark's first personal taxation, its collection enforced by brutal bailiffs who toured the kingdom. The outraged Danes reacted strongly, forcing Knud to flee Jutland. He was pursued, caught and murdered in Odense. **Erik I** completed Knud's work by separating the Danish church from the Hamburg bishop. Erik also introduced a tithe system which both maintained the church's independence and allowed churches to be built of stone rather than wood.

Freed from German influence, Denmark entered a period of stability, but this was rudely shattered by civil war between claimants to the throne which lasted almost 20 years until **Valdemar I** finally united a country grown weary by a generation of bloodshed.

The Valdemars and the Kalmar Union

The country Valdemar I inherited was not only weary but impoverished, since raids into Denmark by the Wends, a Slavic tribe, had increased during the time of civil war. With the help of Bishop Absalon of Roskilde (a warlike cleric who founded Copenhagen in 1167), Valdemar pushed the Wends back, using the treasures looted from Wend cities to advance Danish influence. Ultimately Denmark controlled the Baltic coast as far as Estonia and the mainland south to the Elbe, giving it control of all major trading centres. Valdemar introduced the country's first written laws, the **Jyske Lov** (Jutland Code). These laws were extended by Valdemar's successors, and by the 14th century Denmark was one of Europe's most progressive countries with laws forbidding imprisonment without just cause and a national council with real power.

In 1363 Norway's king **Haakon** – the Norwegians having become independent following the collapse of the northern empire – married **Margrethe**, the daughter of Valdemar IV. Their son, **Olaf**, became king of Denmark in 1375 when Valdemar died, and king of Norway in 1380 on Haakon's death. Olaf was both young and sick – he died aged 17 – so Margrethe ruled the two countries

Opposite: *A rune stone at Jelling – a reminder of Denmark's Viking past.*
Below: *The statue of Knud the Holy at the site of his murder in Odense.*

THE DOCTOR
AND THE QUEEN

Christian VII (1766–1808), suffered from bouts of insanity and came to rely on his doctor, the German Johan Struensee, both for medical help and assistance with government. Struensee, not only took over the running of the country, but also replaced the king in the bed of his 18-year-old queen, Caroline Matilda, the sister of England's George III. Struensee was a reformer, introducing many acts which benefited the country's poor, but was hated by the Danish nobility who rightly feared he wished to see an end to them. With help from Christian's mother, Struensee was arrested and tried for his adulterous relationship with the queen. Caroline Matilda was sent back to Britain, Struensee was sent to the scaffold.

Below: *Looking towards the centre of Copenhagen from the top of the Rundetårn (Round Tower).*

as regent. After the formation of the Kalmar Union Margrethe was the real power in Scandinavia despite her nephew Erik being king.

Erik made Copenhagen his capital, but this shrewd move was undermined by his unsuccessful attack on the Hanseatic League and his enthusiasm for appointing Danes to influential Kalmar positions. Enthusiasm for the Union quickly waned and in 1523 when Sweden elected its own king it ended, though Norway continued to be part of the Danish Kingdom.

Lutheranism, Monarchy and Reform

In 1533 civil war broke out in Denmark when, following the death of Frederik I, who had allowed Lutheran preachers into the country, the Catholic church refused to crown his son, Christian, as king. Christian was a Lutheran and the Catholic bishops rightly feared an end to their wealth and influence. The bishops tried to hand the throne to Hans, Christian's younger brother, but the war went against them. Christian was crowned, Catholic properties were forfeited to the state and **Danish Lutheranism** became the official religion. With the country stable again and its fortunes enriched by the Catholic church treasures, Denmark prospered, but the prosperity was rudely interrupted when a later King Christian (Christian IV) declared war on Sweden. The war, the Thirty Years' War, was a protracted disaster. Sweden invaded Denmark in 1645, forcing Christian IV to cede the island of Gotland and parts of Norway. Then, in 1657, Sweden invaded again, marching an army through Germany into Jutland then across the frozen sea – the winter of 1657–58 is claimed to have been the coldest in Danish history – towards

Copenhagen. Christian's successor, Frederik III, was forced to sign the Treaty of Roskilde which reduced Danish territory by one third. Apart from Schleswig-Holstein, which was to remain under the Danish crown until the 1840s, only the island of Bornholm, which revolted against Swedish rule in 1660, was ever to return to Denmark.

Despite the disaster, Frederik III's own position was enhanced, the king granting himself **absolute power** in 1665. Absolute monarchy resulted in the construction of many of Denmark's finest buildings, but fortuitously Danish kings who were aware of the excesses of power came to the throne in time to prevent the ideas of the French Revolution spreading to Denmark. Land holdings were reformed and, later, compulsory education for children under 14 was introduced. The lot of the ordinary Dane was improved, but unfortunately further reforms were curtailed as Denmark became caught up in the Napoleonic Wars.

Above: *Rosenborg Slot, named for the rose gardens which surround it, was once the home of the Danish royal family.*

The Napoleonic Wars

During the American War of Independence Denmark joined Prussia, Russia and Sweden in an armed neutrality pact aimed at safeguarding trade with both sides in the conflict. The British were not pleased and, when war broke out between Britain and France, the Danes were pressured into abandoning their neutral stance. At first Denmark concurred but, faced with losing trade (Copenhagen was now a major port: indeed, what Britain feared, in part, was the growth of Danish commerce which threatened its own control of the seas), the Danes made another pact with Russia and Sweden. Britain reacted immediately, sending a fleet to Copenhagen which battered the Danish navy. The Danes withdrew from the pact.

ABSOLUTE MONARCHY

After Frederik III's decree of absolute monarchy the Danish monarch's power was so total that when Christian V ascended to the throne in 1670 he decreed that no one other than himself had the right to crown a king and so placed the crown on his own head at his coronation.

Though the action of 1801 hardly endeared the Danes to Britain, Denmark seems mainly to have been interested in staying out of the war and maintaining its trade links. Unfortunately that stance further alienated the British who feared Napoleon would soon capture Copenhagen and control Baltic trade. To forestall that, **Horatio Nelson** sailed a fleet to Copenhagen in 1807, bombarding the city and capturing the entire Danish fleet. The appalled Danes promptly sided with France. Britain blockaded Danish and Norwegian waters, forcing once wealthy Denmark into bankruptcy and poverty, and causing famine in Norway. When the war ended, Denmark was forced to cede Norway to Sweden which had not only stayed neutral, but blocked Danish attempts to change sides when it saw that Napoleon's days were numbered.

The Prussian War

Ironically, Denmark emerged from the dark days of defeat to a dawn of intellectual achievement. Philosopher **Søren Kierkegaard**, writer **Hans Christian Andersen** and sculptor **Bertel Thorvaldsen** were the leaders of a cultural renaissance. In 1849 Frederik VII formally renounced absolute monarchy, a constitution was drawn up and a parliament convened. An independent judiciary was established and the Danes were granted extensive human rights. All the news was not good, however, as Jutland's southern border became the subject of dispute with the Prussia of Bismarck. Holstein, with a largely German population, allied itself with the Germanic states of Prussia in 1840, but Denmark was determined to hold on to Schleswig in which Danes as well as Germans lived. In 1864 Bismarck settled the issue by declaring war on Denmark, seizing Schleswig and redrawing Jutland's border along a line south of **Kolding**.

GREENLAND AND THE FAROES

Although Denmark lost Norway at the end of the Napoleonic Wars, it retained Iceland, the Faroes and Greenland. Ultimately Iceland became independent but Greenland and the Faroes have remained Danish. The Faroes, populated with Viking settlers, was given home rule in 1948. The position in Greenland is less straightforward as there are indigenous Greenlanders with no historic ties to Denmark. Danish interest in the world's biggest island dates from Hans Egede's attempts to find Viking survivors. The island was granted home rule in 1979.

The 20th Century

Northern Schleswig was regained by Denmark after World War I, when a plebiscite in 1920 allowed the chiefly Danish population to vote in favour of the return of southern Jutland to the Danish crown. Denmark declared its neutrality in World War II (as it had in 1914), but Nazi Germany, needing naval bases in northern Jutland, invaded on 9 April 1940, not only marching across the Jutland border, but attacking other strategic sites, including an airfield close to Copenhagen. The Germans delivered an ultimatum to King Christian X and his government – surrender or see Copenhagen bombed. With no hope of resisting, the Danes surrendered. At first Denmark was allowed a certain autonomy, but in August 1943 the Nazis took complete control. The Danish resistance movement then responded, most notably by ensuring the successful evacuation of some 95% of Jews remaining in Denmark to neutral Sweden, by fishing boat at night.

In postwar Europe Denmark became a symbol of the socially conscious state, its welfare programme the envy of left-leaning governments. It also combined this concern for the citizen with unparalleled prosperity and took a European lead in liberalism. In 1967 censorship was outlawed. Despite the vociferous complaints (both inside and outside the country) that the level of sex crimes would increase and society would degenerate, the Danes took it all in their stride. If anything, the liberalization has led to a reduction in sex-based crime. Denmark also allowed the Christiania experiment (*see* panel, this page). Denmark joined the European Economic Community (now the European Union) in 1973, but the Danes have shown an independence of spirit which has exasperated both European and their own politicians. Demanding referenda on important issues, the Danes voted against the Maastricht Treaty (which proposed greater economic and political union) in 1992,

CHRISTIANIA

In 1971 an old military base near Christianshavn was invaded by hippies protesting at the arms race and rampant capitalism. Despite the misgivings of many (which continue to this day) the government allowed the setting up of 'Free Christiania', a self-governing enclave. The population of the 'state' is about 1000 and has proved itself responsible by outlawing 'hard' drugs, in exchange for which the police turn a blind eye to the sale of marijuana.

Opposite: *The memorial to the battle of Koge Bay near the Kastellet.*
Below: *The 'free city' of Christiania, the 'hippy state' across the water from Copenhagen's main centre.*

Below: *The Dannebrog, Denmark's flag. Danes are immensely proud of their flag: legend has it that God presented it to them.*

accepting the Treaty with certain exemptions in a second referendum in 1993. Then, despite a massive government campaign in favour, the country voted against joining the Euro (the EU's common currency) in September 2000.

GOVERNMENT AND ECONOMY

Denmark is a constitutional monarchy; **Queen Margrethe II**, who ascended the throne in 1972, is head of state. Her position is ceremonial, although no new legislation can be enacted without her signature. The government has a single-chamber parliament, the **Folketing**, of 179 seats, headed by a prime minister and appointed cabinet. There are two main political parties: the left-leaning Socialdemokratiat (Social Democrats) and the right-of-centre Venstre (Liberals). Any party winning 2% of the popular vote is entitled to a seat (or seats) in parliament. One recent major development is the rise of the Dansk Folkeparti, a right-wing party opposed to further immigration into Denmark and further integration with the European Union. The voting age in Denmark is 18.

The Danish **economy** is still based largely on agri-culture, and over 60% of the country's land area is given over to farming. Cereals and oil-seed rape are grown, for export as well as home consumption, while livestock farming underpins a famous export market in dairy products, bacon and canned ham. The latter often puzzles visitors as it is possible to tour the Danish countryside for days without ever spotting a pig. Fishing is also important, and Danish trawlers work the Baltic and North seas for catches which are either for the table or the pro-duction of fish meal.

Denmark is famous for design, and there is a thriving export trade in electronic goods, furni-ture, porcelain and glass. The Danish economy is one of the soundest in Europe, the GNP

being the highest, per capita, in the EU. To this must be added a welfare system which is one of the most all-embracing in Europe, paid for by high taxation (both direct, income tax, and indirect, VAT) which the Danes accept as a requirement for a socially aware and cohesive country.

THE PEOPLE

Denmark has a population of about 5.3 million. Of these 1.75 million live in Copenhagen and about 260,000 in Århus. Altogether, about 70% of all Danes live in towns. About 95% of the population is Danish, the other 5% being immigrants (an increase of about threefold since the 1970s). Danes see themselves as an environmentally conscious, culturally sophisticated folk – and are quite right to do so. They are less sure of being seen as Scandinavians. Without a midnight sun or skiing heritage, they are not keen to be lumped together with Swedes and Norwegians. Though proud of their Viking past, they now consider themselves to be European rather than a fringe nation.

The Danish character is dominated by **hygge** and **janteloven**, both of which are difficult to translate as they are more an attitude of mind than anything easily defined. *Hygge* (pronounced hoog-a) means 'cosy', but cosy is a physical attribute whereas *hygge* is more spiritual. It is to be comfortable with, at one with, another person or persons. To describe someone as *hygge* is a great compliment as it means they are good company in a gentle, convivial way. *Janteloven*, meaning 'Jante's law', derives from a 1930s book by the writer Aksel Sandemose set in Jante, a fictional Jutland town. Sandemose used the book to expose what he saw as an unenviable trait in his countrymen of wanting to drag everyone down to the same level. This small-mindedness he set down in ten laws – do not assume you are better than anyone else, do not assume you will achieve anything of value – which, he claimed, dominated the life of Jante folk. Though widely decried as an old misery, Sandemose had put his finger on

Above: *Danes like sea bathing, despite the temperature of the water.*

LANGUAGE

Danish derives from the Viking language, a heritage shared by the Swedish and Norwegians. Danes, Swedes and Norwegians understand each other, but can't understand Icelanders as Icelandic is virtually the unchanged Viking tongue, unadulterated by the influences of neighbouring cultures.

SOME NUMBERS

zero	0	*nul*
one	1	*en*
two	2	*to*
three	3	*tre*
four	4	*fire*
five	5	*fem*
six	6	*seks*
seven	7	*syv*
eight	8	*otte*
nine	9	*ni*
ten	10	*ti*
hundred	100	*hundrede*
thousand	1000	*tusind*

Above: *This untitled painting by Asgar Jorn is in the new Louisiana Gallery.*

a Danish character trait that is still much in evidence. *Janteloven* has been seen by many – including Queen Margrethe who has often spoken out against it – as being a self-defeating philosophy, one that negates attempts at excellence and self-improvement. To the visitor Denmark may seem to have shaken itself free of *janteloven*, but in reality the ideas behind the 'laws' are still much in evidence. Often when speaking of someone who has done well – received a promotion or award – you will hear a famous Danish proverb quoted: 'The higher a monkey climbs, the more you see of its bottom'.

Religion

Denmark has a state-supported church, the **Lutheran Folkekirken** (People's Church). This claims the support of 90% of Danes, though statistics reveal that less than 5% regularly attend services.

The Artists

Until the early 19th century most Danish art was portraiture, almost exclusively of the royal family and aristocracy. At that time the work of **Christoffer Willelm Eckersberg** and his pupil **Christen Købke** introduced a school of realism which has been admired and copied ever since. Købke in particular has become internationally famous in recent years. In the 20th century the **COBRA** movement (from Copenhagen-Brussels-Amsterdam), which accentuates free expression, dominated Danish painting though few artists have acquired an international reputation. Perhaps the most famous are **Asgar Jorn**, who died in 1973, and **Per Kirkeby**, who still produces influential art.

In sculpture **Bertel Thorvaldsen** (1770–1844) is still considered the finest artist Denmark has produced. His art, heavily influenced by classical Greek and Roman sculpture, can be seen in a museum in Copenhagen devoted to his work (*see* page 43). A new generation of artists is now introducing conceptual art to Denmark, notably **Olafur Eliasson**, whose work mixes high art and engineering.

In literature Denmark has had a greater influence on the world. **Hans Christian Andersen**'s stories have been translated into almost every language and have been an introduction to literature for generations of children. **Karen Blixen** was twice nominated for literature's Nobel Prize and many believe she should have won it: indeed, it is said that Ernest Hemingway, who did win it in one of her nomination years, told her she deserved it more than he. Three Danes have won the award – in 1917 the poet **Karl Gjellerup** and novelist **Henrik Pontoppidan** shared it, while the poet **Johannes Jensen** won in 1944. Of modern novelists **Peter Høeg** has recently won international fame for *Miss Smilla's Feeling for Snow* (*see* panel, page 55).

Denmark's best-known classical composer is **Carl Nielsen** (1865–1931) whose music includes six symphonies and several operas. Nielsen also wrote hymns and popular songs. Today **Per Nørgård** and **Paul Ruders** continue to bring Danish classical music to an international audience. Denmark has also produced excellent jazz musicans, but only after the ECM record label brought Scandinavian artists to prominence did Danish players, such as bass player **Niels-Herring Pedersen** and trumpeter **Thomas Fryland**, become internationally well known.

Architecturally **Niels (Nicolai) Eigtved** must take pride of place for his work in Copenhagen in the early 18th century, his rococo work defining the city we now see. **Arne Jacobsen** and **Kaare Klint** must also be mentioned as in addition to their architectural work they defined a design ethos which still dominates: that form follows function. It is that simple axiom which has made Danish design and designers so sought after.

THE DAISY ROUTE

Those who tour Denmark by car, motorcycle or even bicycle will soon see the sign of a marguerite (the ox-eye daisy, Denmark's national flower) against a brown background. This denotes the Marguerite or Daisy Route, an interlocking series of roads – usually secondary or minor roads – which, over a distance of 3500km (2175 miles) link the most important historic sites in the country by way of particular scenic routes. A guide book to the route is published in Danish, English and German. Though following the entire route would be a *tour de force*, visitors with a little time to spare in any area will find the Daisy Route a welcome change from the high-speed charge along the motorway.

Below: *The Black Diamond, Copenhagen's controversial Royal Library building.*

DOGME 95

Denmark has a remarkable pedigree in film-making dating from the early years of the medium, the work of Lau Lauritsen and, especially, Carl Theodore Dryer being highly influential. Then in 1995 four young directors, of whom Lars Von Trier is the most famous (or infamous in certain eyes), published the DOGME 95 Manifesto which identified criteria for making 'real' films as opposed to what they saw as the excesses of Hollywood. The 10 'Vows' of DOGME 95 included location only shooting (no props or sets), hand-held cameras, no special lighting or effects, and no dubbing. Von Trier's *Breaking the Waves* was heralded by many as a masterpiece although his 2000 Cannes prize-winning *Dancer in the Dark* starring Björk was slated and admired in equal measures.

SPORT

Danes enjoy all sports, but as a relatively small nation find world domination difficult. They excel at football, the national team often performing far above the level expected of a nation of just 5 million. In 1992, having failed to qualify for the European Championship they slipped into the event as first reserve when the Balkan conflict meant Yugoslavia could not travel and won it, beating Germany 2–0 in the final, a result that enraptured the nation.

The Scientists

Whether philosophy is an art or a science is still a matter of debate, but either way the name of **Søren Kierkegaard**, 'the founding father of existentialism', will be mentioned. Kierkegaard's philosophy was a contradiction of the work of Hegel, believing that the individual was required to make his/her choices alone from those on offer. Though this might appear to be at odds with a religious outlook, Kierkegaard was a man of faith. He believed that man's existence was divided into the aesthetic, the ethical and the religious and that only by leading a truly Christian life could peace be found. Many believe that the deep pain of a broken engagement is the basis of Kierkegaard's beliefs. He died, exhausted by a bitter dispute with the Danish church, at the age of 42.

Niels Bohr is the most famous of Danish scientists, widely referred to as the father of atomic science. His model of the atom is still taught as the basis of atomic theory. Recently, Bohr's conversation with the German physicist Werner Heisenburg regarding the Nazi atom bomb programme has been the subject of much debate and also of the play *Copenhagen*. Bohr won the Nobel Physics Prize in 1922, and Bohr's son **Aage** won the same prize in 1975 (with co-worker **Ben Mottelson** and

American **James Rainwater**) for work on the atomic nucleus. In addition to these prizes Danish scientists have also been Nobel Laureates in Chemistry (**Jens Skou**, with two Americans, in 1997 for work on cellular energy storage) and in physiology/ medicine (**Niels Finsen** in 1903, **Auguste Krogh** in 1920, **Johannes Fibiger** in 1926, **Henrik Dam** in 1943 and **Niels Jerne** in 1984), a remarkable record for such a small nation, and a record to which the 1908 Peace Prize can be added, **Frederik Bajer** having won for his work as an activist and writer.

Food and Drink

The essence of Danish cooking is fish, meat and potatoes, often with cabbage. The meat will usually be pork (*flæskesteg* – roast pork, usually with potatoes and cabbage; *frikadeller* – pork meatballs, often with potatoes and red cabbage) or beef (*fyldt hvidkålshoved* – ground beef in cabbage leaves; *hvid labskovs* – beef stew). The fish will be one of a multitude of types, though cod (*kogt torsk* – poached cod), plaice and salmon are popular. Herring is the basis of the *koldt bord*, the cold table, a Danish breakfast and lunch speciality. Herring can be pickled or salted and is often eaten with raw onion, a mix which, at breakfast, is claimed to set the stomach up for the day but which (speaking personally) is more likely to do just the opposite. The other Danish speciality is smørrebrød, the open sandwich topped with shrimps or cold meats and a mountain of salad.

Above: *Denmark is famous for its beers.*
Opposite: *Herring is a Danish speciality.*

Denmark has no wine industry, but does brew both Carlsberg and Tuborg, the former with what is probably the most imitated advertising line in the world. Spirits include Heering's famous cherry liqueur and akvavit, a potent drink chiefly distilled in Aalborg. Akvavit comes in many flavours and is customarily downed in one. Danes often follow pickled herring and raw onion with akvavit (a combination which seems near lethal).

LANGUAGE TIPS
soup • *suppa*
bread • *brød*
fish • *fisk*
meat • *kød*
coffee • *kaffe*
I am a vegetarian
• *Jeg er vegetar*
tea • *te*
milk • *mælk*
beer • *øl*
wine • *vin*
cheers • *skål*
Monday • *mandag*
Tuesday • *tirsdag*
Wednesday • *onsdag*
Thursday • *torsdag*
Friday • *fredag*
Saturday • *lørdag*
Sunday • *søndag*

2
Copenhagen

The most casual glance at a map of Denmark is enough to suggest that the country's capital should be on Fyn, the central island, or perhaps on Jutland, Denmark's biggest landmass. Copenhagen, which is situated at the extreme eastern side of Zealand, is just too far away from the rest of the country to be a sensible place for a capital.

When the country was first unified under Gorm and Harald Bluetooth the capital was Jelling, at the heart of Jutland. At that time, where Copenhagen now stands, there was a tiny port set where the Baltic swept through a narrow channel dividing a small island from the Zealand coast. It was called **Havn**, harbour, a simple name that reflected its sheltered nature. From the little port, set among boggy salt marshes, men sailed to fish the herring of Øresund. So numerous were the fish, it was said, that nets weren't needed to catch them. All a man had to do was put his hands in the water and scoop them out. Then, as now, herring was the staple diet of the Danes, but rich though the waters off Havn were, the place was still just a fishing port and was ignored by the royal masters of Denmark as they struggled for power on Jutland.

In about 1160 **Valdemar I** gave the area around Havn to **Bishop Absalon** as part of the campaign to rid Zealand of attacks by the Wends. In 1167 Absalon built a fort at Slotsholmen, on a piece of land where the fishermen had dried their nets. That date is now celebrated as the official founding of the city. As Absalon's town grew, its importance as a Baltic trading port became recognized, particularly after Denmark's influence expanded east-

Don't Miss

*** **Tivoli:** great fun for all the family. Good restaurants. Wonderful at Christmas.
*** **Nyhavn:** the most picturesque place in town. Terrific on a summer evening.
*** **National Museum:** stunning collection; good shop and café too.
*** **Ny Carlsberg Glyptotek:** another fine collection, with a good shop and café.
** **Strøget:** long pedestrianized shopping street.
* **The Little Mermaid:** worth the walk, but no one will believe you if you don't go.

Opposite: *Anton Rosen's statue of Viking lur players is a symbol of Copenhagen.*

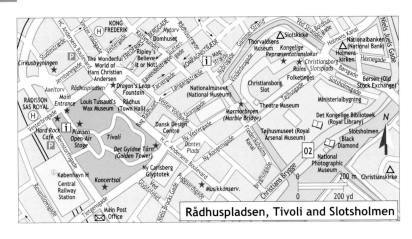

Rådhuspladsen, Tivoli and Slotsholmen

wards following the defeat of the Wends. The number of merchants' houses in the city increased, and they also altered its name, Havn becoming **Købmandshavn** – 'merchant's harbour' – shortened to **København**.

Not only did the city attract a name change, but the jealous attentions of the Hanseatic League: Copenhagen was attacked in 1249 and its harbour was blocked by scuttled ships during a later raid. The city responded by improving its defences and expanding still further, though it was not until 1417, when Erik VII took control of the city away from the church and settled there permanently, that Copenhagen became the capital of Denmark.

By the early 18th century the city had a population of around 65,000, but almost a third of them died when plague struck. A great fire in 1728 razed half the city, destroying much of the squalor that had allowed plague to reign rampant. From the ashes rose a new city, one laid out on the expansive lines that combine the needs of a great capital with those of the people who inhabit it. Copenhagen was European City of Culture in 1996, a good choice for this most sophisticated of cities.

RÅDHUSPLADSEN ★★★

Visitors arriving by plane usually take the high-speed rail link into the city, arriving at the Central Station and emerging on to Tietgensgade or, occasionally, Bernstorffsgade. These two streets enclose two sides of Tivoli. Walking along either and rounding a corner brings the first view of **Rådhuspladsen**, the Town Hall Square. The square was part of the original Havn and, later, site of the city's eastern gate. Now traffic-free, but not free of countless hopeful hawkers, fast-food kiosks and visitors trying to get their bearings, the square is the heart of Copenhagen. A constant stream of city folk cross it, heading for Strøget or the bus and train stations (the bus station is on the square), while on all sides stand buildings which hallmark the city as a western capital, a point reinforced at night by the neon signs.

On its southeastern side the square is close to the **Rådhus**, the Town Hall, completed in 1905 to a design by Martin Nyrop whose bust, together with those of three other famous city sons (Niels Bohr, Hans Christian Andersen and Bertel Thorvaldsen), adorns the central hall. These can by viewed, as can the complex of corridors and stately rooms, during guided tours (Mon–Fri at 15:00, Sat

JENS OLSEN'S CLOCK

Jens Olsen (1872–1945) was a noted astro-mechanic, his world clock taking 27 years to construct and not being started until 10 years after his death. The clock cost 1 million kroner to build and has to be wound each week. One wheel turns every 10 seconds, but another will not complete a full revolution for 26,000 years.

Below: *The Rådhus, which fills one side of the pedestrianized section of Rådhuspladsen. The central (gold) statue is of Bishop Absalon.*

BISHOP ABSALON

Absalon was born in about 1128, the child of an influential Zealand family. He was raised by the royal family, becoming a 'brother' of the boy who would become Valdemar I. Absalon was responsible for most of the accounts of his own life and so comes out of them well – educated, a devout Christian (Bishop of Roskilde from 1157) and great military leader. He was influential in the defeat of the Wends, his reducing of a sacred wooden statue to fire-wood being the symbol of victory. After Valdemar's death Absalon was the effective ruler of Denmark until his own death in 1201. He is buried at Sorø in central Zealand.

at 12:00). Tours also reach the top of the 105.6m (346.5ft) Town Hall Tower (by lift or 300 steps according to taste and fitness), second only to that on the Christiansborg Slot (which is all of 40cm/16in taller) in the list of Danish towers (tours Jun–Sep Mon–Fri 10:00, 12:00 and 14:00, Sat 12:00; Oct–May Mon–Sat 12:00). Also in the Rådhus is **Jens Olsens Verdensur** – Jens Olsen's world clock with over 19,000 individual parts indicating local, solar and sidereal time and the times of sunrise and sunset as well as calendar and planetary data. The red-brick façade of the Rådhus is enlivened by an array of whimsical gargoyles and figures, but is dominated by a golden statue of Bishop Absalon. This is set above a balcony on which the Danish football team appeared before a rapturous crowd after their victory in the 1992 European Championships.

To the right of the Rådhus (when viewing it from the square) is a statue of a seated **Hans Christian Andersen**. As the statue is set beside HC Andersens Boulevard it is very aptly positioned, but seems rather tucked away for so famous a Dane. The near-

by **Dragon's Leap Fountain** by Joachim Skovgaard is much more prominent (and, to be fair, more impressive). The stone pillar near it is Denmark's 'zero point': all distances to the capital are measured from this point.

Just behind the Rådhus is the **Dansk Design Centre** designed by Henning Larsen. The centre opened in 2000 as a means of bringing Danish design to the world. The building was to have had a liquid crystal wall that could act as a giant screen, but that proved too costly, much to

Larsen's dismay. The centre houses a permanent collection (chiefly of furniture) and also temporary exhibitions on companies at the sharp end of Danish design. The café in the entrance lobby is a good place for a coffee (open Mon–Fri 10:00–17:00, Wed 10:00–21:00; Sat, Sun and holidays 11:00–16:00). Across HC Andersens Boulevard from the Rådhus is **Louis Tussaud's Wax Museum**, opened in 1974. There is a collection of celebrities, and famous Danes, as well as the ubiquitous Chamber of Horrors. Most of the wax figures are unconvincing and the horrors lacking in horror – a by-product of the television age? – but the place does have an old-world quaintness (open Apr–Sep daily 10:00–22:00; Oct–Mar daily 10:00–17:00).

Above: *One of the many attractions in Tivoli.*
Opposite: *The bank of slogans, illuminated at night, where Vesterbrogade leaves Rådhuspladsen marks Copenhagen out as a capital city.*

In much the same category as the waxworks is **Ripley's Believe It or Not!** across Vester Voldgade from the Rådhuspladsen, close to the lur players (*see* panel, page 13), where the usual selection of oddities and not-really-so-oddities has been collected into another of US showman Robert Ripley's chain of freak shows (open Jun–Aug daily 10:00–22:00; Sep–May daily 10:00–18:00, but Fri and Sat until 20:00). Close by, the wonderful world of Hans Christian Andersen at Rådhuspladensen opened to celebrate the 200th anniversary of the writer's birth. Open daily 10:00–17:00. The museum is next door to Ripley's Believe It or Not!

AROUND TIVOLI ★★★

It is said that when, in 1841, King Christian VIII was concerned about the growing unrest among ordinary Danes over the principle of absolute monarchy he suggested the building of an amusement park to give the populace

Above: *The sign for Tivoli, seen from Rådhuspladsen. At night the fireworks light up just like the real thing for an eye-catching display.*

something to take their minds off the topic. If this story is true – and though deeply politically incorrect in today's climate, the king was only repeating the 'bread and circuses' idea that had been around for centuries – then despite the sentiments, the Danes have much for which to thank the king. Today **Tivoli**, the park Christian envisaged, is not only the country's most popular amusement park, but a national monument. It is almost a part of the Danish psyche, a place that embodies the essence of *hygge* (open mid-Apr to Sep Sun–Thu 11:00–23:00, Fri and Sat 11:00–00:30; the park also opens 11:00–23:00 for one week before Christmas).

The park was the brainchild of **Georg Carstensen**, who had already funded temporary funfairs in Kongens Nytorv and was keen to find a permanent site. The site chosen was then outside the city, Copenhagen having since expanded to engulf it. Carstensen's idea was to base all the individual parts on one or another (or a combination of) music, lights and fantasy. King Christian added a proviso that there should be nothing degrading. The chosen name mirrors that of the gardens in Paris, which itself derives from the town near Rome famous for its fountains. Copenhagen's Tivoli opened on 15 August 1843 and one of the 16,000 who visited that day was, fittingly in view of the design idea, Hans Christian Andersen. He must have been impressed, as now are most of the 5 million annual visitors, many of them Danes, their repeat visits swelling the numbers.

The basic design of the park has changed little in over 160 years of its existence, nor has its curious mix of the highbrow and the lowbrow – fine restaurants and fast food, classical music and rock concerts, theatre and night-

---

THE UNFORGETTABLE GEORG CARSTENSEN

It is claimed that when Georg Carstensen returned to Denmark after a self-imposed exile in the USA he was made to pay to enter Tivoli by an unimpressed attendant who neither recognized nor believed him. To this humiliation is added another (though in this the designer is not alone) – Carstensen's statue is a regular perch for birds.

club, fantasy-based architecture and the down-to-earth delights of a real funfair. The main entrance, in classical style, is in Vesterbrogade. Just inside is the moghul-like **Restaurant Nimb** in front of which is the **Bubble Fountain** designed by the great Danish physicist Niels Bohr (the statue is taken down at the end of the summer season to protect it from frost damage: when the park opens at Christmas the space in front of the Nimb is filled with a Christmas tree). The Nimb is one of 37 restaurants which cater for all tastes and pockets. At the heart of the park is a lake, surrounded by beautiful trees and gardens, on which floats a galleon-restaurant. Close to it is **Plænen** open-air stage where shows vary from ballet through circus to rock concerts. The **Peacock Theatre**, the oldest theatre in Tivoli, is the venue for pantomime and ballet-pantomime. The vast peacock tail folds away to reveal the stage. Almost as exotic, and echoing the Oriental theme, is the **Chinese Pagoda** in front of which there is an open-air ice-skating rink at Christmas. The **Koncertsal**, at the far end of the park from the main entrance, is the venue for concerts which frequently include world-famous artists. Close by is a statue of a slightly bemused Georg Carstensen. Beside the concert hall is a roller coaster. In the opposite corner is **Det Gyldne Tårn** (the Golden Tower), added when it was realized that the roller coaster (daring in its day but now seen as rather pedestrian) and ferris wheel (delightful, with little hot-air balloons 'supporting' the seats) were a little tame for 21st-century teenagers.

Though Tivoli is an all-day venue, to really appreciate Georg Carstensen's vision it is necessary to come at night when a hundred thousand lights create a real fairy-tale atmosphere. There are fireworks displays on

---

THE GOLDEN TOWER

One of the best views over Copenhagen is that from the top of Tivoli's **Det Gyldne Tårn** (the Golden Tower). The tower is 63m (207ft) high and from the top, at night, the lights of Malmö, in Sweden, can be seen across Øresund. But there is a drawback, one which might make you think twice about taking your camera. The tower is one of Tivoli's favourite rides, the seats that take riders to the top dropping under gravity, a rush preceded by an alarming hiss and so sudden that stomachs (and, possibly, cameras) are left behind.

Below: *At Christmas the whole of Tivoli is decked with lights.*

THE GLYPTOTEK'S
WINTER GARDEN

Just beyond the entrance of Ny
Carlsberg Glyptotek is a terrific
glass-domed Winter Garden,
which belies its name by
being a greenhouse of tropical
plants set around a curious,
surreal fountain by Kai
Nielsen. There is a good café
here too.

Opposite: *Vor Frue Kirke,*
the Church of Our Lady,
stands on one of the oldest
Christian sites in the city.
Below: *The Caritas*
(Charity) in Strøget is one
of Copenhagen's best-
loved fountains.

Wednesdays and Saturdays during the summer: the displays can't really compare with the Tivoli lights.

Across Tietgensgade from Tivoli is **Ny Carlsberg
Glyptotek**, the Carlsberg sculpture collection. In 1888
Carl Jacobsen, son of the founder of the Carlsberg
brewery, gave his collection of classical art to the city, and
Vilhelm Dahlerup and Hack Kampmann designed
a building worthy of so generous a benefaction. The
collection explores the history of Middle Eastern and
European sculpture from the Stone Age to the Greek and
Roman periods, and also includes 18th- and 19th-century
works, notably by Rodin and Degas (a complete set of
bronzes). There is also a fine collection of work by Danish
sculptors and a collection of Impressionist paintings with
many by Gauguin (who was married to a Dane and lived
in Copenhagen before heading for Tahiti), as well as can-
vases by Monet, Cezanne, Van Gogh and other famous
names of the school (open Tue–Sun 10:00–16:00).

STRØGET **

Heading northeast from Rådhuspladsen is Strøget, though
the visitor who looks for this name on the wall-mounted
street-name plates can spend fruitless minutes. Strøget
(stripe) is a 1.5km (1-mile) pedestrianized road which
actually comprises a total of five streets (namely Nygade,
Frederiksberggade, Vimmel-
skaftet, Amagertorv and
Østergade), together with
the two squares which lie
along the way, that link
Rådhuspladsen to Kongens
Nytorv. Strøget is Copen-
hagen's main shopping
street. All the big names of
world shopping are here, as
well as the cream of Danish
shopping and some of the
city's best cafés and clubs.
The little side streets on
either side of Strøget are

well worth exploring as some of the best shops, cafés, etc. spill into these streets.

Frederiksberggade is the most touristy – and always the most crowded – part of Strøget. In streets to the left are some of the city's best and cheapest clothing shops for young people as well as record shops, lively cafés, etc., all grouped close to part of Copenhagen University. **Club Absalon** is built on the site of Bishop Absalon's first church (the last sections of which can be seen in the bar toilets!). The first square is actually two – **Gammeltorv**, left, and **Nytorv**, right – each one cobbled and very pretty. Gammeltorv is the city's oldest square. At its centre is the **Caritas Fountain**, which dates from 1608 making it one of the oldest of

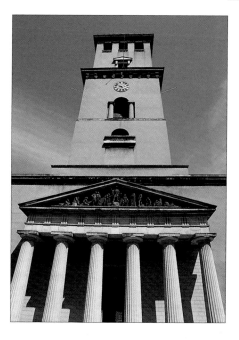

its type in Europe. The moving work (*caritas* means charity) is in copper and depicts a pregnant woman and two children. The fountain was the centrepiece of Copenhagen's main market square at the time. Today, flower-sellers and peddlers of more chancy wares move among the tourists. Nytorv is dominated by the **Damhuset**, the early 19th-century Courthouse. Turn left through Gammeltorv to reach **Vor Frue Kirke** (the Church of Our Lady), built after the 1807 British bombardment destroyed what was itself only the latest in a series of churches on the site, the first having been erected in 1191.

Another fine church, **Helligåndskirken** (Church of the Holy Spirit), lies ahead and left. It dates from the early 15th century. In **Amagertorv** there is a **Tobacco Museum**, to the right (open Mon–Thu 10:00–18:00, Fri 10:00–19:00, Sat 10:00–17:00), then the second square, **Højbro Plads**, in the lower part of which stands a statue of Bishop Absalon depicting the warrior cleric on horseback.

NIELS BOHR, FATHER OF THE ATOM

The famous scientist was on the staff at Copenhagen University and a (possibly apocryphal) tale records that a visitor once noticed a horse-shoe hanging in his office. Surprised that so rational a man could believe in such lucky charms, the visitor questioned Bohr who replied that he didn't believe in such things, but had been told that they worked even if you didn't.

Above: *The National Museum, one of the undoubted highlights of the city.*

Beyond the bishop is Slotsholmen where he built the city's first fortress. Amagertorv also has a fountain, **Storkespringvandet**, the Stork Fountain. Close by is **Royal Copenhagen**, a recent amalgamation of once independent porcelain, glass and silver shops. Shoppers will see some of the best of Danish design, but will need a deep pocket. The shop's café is excellent (it sells the best hot chocolate in town).

Turning right in Højbro Plads, the visitor soon reaches, to the left, **Sankt Nikolaj Kirke** (St Nicholas' Church), now an exhibition centre and café. A left turn in the square leads to **Købmagergade**, another pedestrianized shopping street. In it, to the left, is a **Post and Telecommunications Museum** (open Tue, Thu–Sat 10:00–17:00, Wed 10:00–20:00, Sun 10:00–16:00), and the rather easier to spot **Museum Erotica** (open May–Sep daily 10:00–23:00; Oct–Apr daily 11:00–20:00). Despite Denmark's liberal stance on censorship (or lack thereof), the museum is not on the city's official list of museums – the equivalent of wrapping an 'adult' magazine in brown paper. The museum itself continues the allusion: its lower floor is instructive and objective, and the upper floor is the equivalent of the top shelf of a newsagent, with a floor-to-ceiling stack of video screens showing hard porn non-stop. Not for the faint-hearted.

Beyond the museums is the **Rundetårn**, the Round Tower, Europe's oldest astronomical observatory, built by Christian IV and opened in 1642. The tower is climbed along a 200m spiral ramp (with a few stairs at the top). In 1716 the Russian Czar Peter the Great rode up the ramp on a horse (his wife following in a horse-drawn carriage). In 1902 a car drove up the ramp. There is a terrific view of the city from the tower's top (open Jun–Aug Mon–Sat 10:00–20:00, Sun 12:00–20:00; Sept–May Mon–Sat 10:00–17:00, Sun 12:00–17:00). The present observatory, at the top, is open to interested visitors at night in winter (open mid-Oct to Mar, Tue and Wed 19:00–22:00).

Back in Strøget the quality shops continue all the way to Kongens Nytorv, with the **Guinness World Records Museum** to the left at the corner of Østergade and Ny Østergade. The museum (like Ripley's Believe It or Not! it is part of a worldwide chain) has the usual collection of curios and weird records – of interest mostly to those who are interested in that sort of thing. Open all year, Mon–Thu and Sun 10:00–18:00, Fri and Sat 10:00–20:00.

SLOTSHOLMEN ★★★

Heading southeast from Rådhuspladsen along Vester Voldgade, a left turn into Ny Vestergade brings you to the elegantly impressive entrance of the **Nationalmuseet** (open all year, Tue–Sun 10:00–17:00). Housed in a former royal palace (built in the 1740s by Niels Eigtved, one of Denmark's most important architects), the museum is a must for all visitors. Through the door is a courtyard that has been roofed in glass to create a light, spacious entranceway. At the far end is a book and gift shop, while the gallery above has a café. The museum concentrates on Danish history, but also has excellent Egyptian, Greek and Roman collections. Ancient Danish history is represented by the collection of bronze lurs, some reputedly still playable, and the famous sun chariot (see page 14). Later items include fine rune stones and wonderful gold pieces from the Viking era, and a memorable collection of artwork from Denmark's medieval period. There is also a quite exceptional children's museum which belies the idea that museums are worthy, but dull.

Continuing along Ny Vestergade the visitor reaches the **Marmor-broen**, the marble bridge.

Below: *Frederiksholms Kanal, dug in the 17th century as part of the city's fortifications.*

TYCHO BRAHE

Considered the greatest astronomer of the pre-telescope era, Tycho Brahe was born in southern Sweden, then under Danish rule, in 1546 and studied astronomy and mathematics at Copenhagen University. He observed a nova in 1572, fixing its position so accurately he could prove it was further than the moon. Frederick II funded the building of an observatory for him. This allowed him to prove that comets circled the sun and were not atmospheric phenomena. In 1596 Brahe moved to Prague where he died in 1601. An arrogant, short-tempered man, he lost most of his nose in a duel while still a student and spent the rest of his life wearing a false nose made of silver.

The bridge crosses the semicircular loop of water that gives the name to **Slotsholmen** – Castle Island. It was here that Bishop Absalon built the fortress from which he campaigned against the Wends. The canal that, moat-like, encircles the island dates from the time of Christian IV, while the little that remains of Absalon's castle has been incorporated into **Christiansborg Slot**, the fourth building on the site, previous castles having been destroyed by fire or the desires of kings. The present building, distinctly more palace than castle, dates from the early 19th century, but required rebuilding in 1884 when it, too, was damaged by fire. It is said that the glow from the blaze could be seen in Jutland.

The castle is now the seat of the Danish parliament, the **Folketinget**. The chamber can be visited by joining a guided tour (in English, daily at 14:00, Sun only in winter). The **Kongelige Repræsentationslokar** (Royal Reception Chambers) can also be visited on a guided tour (May–Sep daily, tours in English at 11:00, 13:00, 15:00). The chambers, hung with tapestries depicting Denmark's history (made by Bjorn Norgard in 1990 to celebrate Queen Margrethe's 50th birthday), are still used for formal occasions. The ruins of Absalon's castle can also be viewed (open May–Sep Mon–Sun 10:00–16:00; Oct–Apr, daily except Mon, 10:00–16:00). The castle has a **theatre museum** housed in the old court theatre (open Tues–Thurs 11:00–15:00, as well as a collection of the royal family's carriages – **Kongelige Stalde og Kareter** – complete with riders' uniforms, saddles, etc. (open May–Sep Fri–Sun 14:00–16:00; Oct–Apr Sat and Sun 14:00–16:00). The latter museum is housed in the castle stables which are still in use, and the horses are exercised in the castle's great courtyards where they are watched over by King Christian IV, in the form of a statue – appropriately enough – on horseback.

To the left of the castle (viewed from the Marble Bridge) is the excellent **Thorvaldsens Museum** (open Tue–Sun 10:00–17:00) dedicated

Stroget and Nyhavn

to the work of Bertel Thorvaldsen, Denmark's greatest sculptor (*see page 26*). Beside it is the **Slotskirke**, the castle church, built in the 1820s in beautiful neoclassical style. On the other side of the castle the **Børsen**, Copenhagen's Old Stock Exchange (the oldest in Europe – the building is now a business centre and not open to the public), is most notable for the twisted spire formed by the plaiting of four dragon's tails. The spire is topped by three crowns – the triple crowns of Denmark, Norway and Sweden.

Across the canal from Børsen is the **Nationalbanken**, Denmark's National Bank, designed by Arne Jacobsen. Beside it is the **Holmenskirken**, built in 1562 as an anchor forge for the Danish Navy, but converted to a church dedicated to sailors in 1619. Queen Margrethe married Prince Henrik here in 1967. On the opposite side of Slotsholmen from the Børsen, the **Tøjhusmuseet** is the Royal Arsenal Museum with a weaponry collection spanning the ages (open Tue–Sun 12:00–16:00). Between the Børsen and the museum is the **Royal Library**, the extension of which building, known locally as the Black Diamond, is the city's most controversial recent addition. Built of polished black granite, it is either impressively modern or hideously out of place, depending on the taste of the individual looking at it. Either way, it certainly cannot be ignored. Apart from a phenomenal book collection (accessible to visitors Mon–Fri 10:00–21:00, Sat 10:00–17:00) and a very good café, the Black Diamond houses the **National Photographic Museum**.

THE MARBLE BRIDGE

Built from 1741–45 in fine rococo style by Nicolai Eigtved (usually called Niels Eigtved), this bridge is much loved by the Danes. Despite its name, little marble was used in the construction, the decorative work mostly being sandstone.

THE CASTLE CHURCH BURNS

In 1884 the Christiansborg church survived a potentially devastating fire, but another in 1992, caused when a Whitsun carnival firework went off course and ignited the roof, resulted in ruinous damage. The building blazed and then collapsed, but miraculously a Bertel Thorvaldsen frieze that ringed the ceiling survived. The church was restored by 1997 and used for the service of celebration for Queen Margrethe's 25th anniversary.

Opposite: *Christiansborg Slot, once the royal palace.*

NYHAVN ★★★

Nyhavn, the new harbour, was dug from 1671–73 to allow ships to reach Kongens Nytorv. After the British bombarded the city in 1807 the merchants whose houses lined the harbour moved out, fearing for their future safety, and the area became Copenhagen's red-light district. It had improved by the time Hans Christian Andersen arrived – he lived at Nos. 18 and 20 before

Above: *In winter the centre of Kongens Nytorv is turned into an outdoor ice-skating rink.*

settling at No. 67 where he lived for 20 years – then gradually transformed itself into the heart of Copenhagen's social (and tourist) scene. It is without doubt the city's prettiest place and one of the most delightful in any European capital. A stroll along the busy north side and then a view of it from the quieter south side is a must. On a sunny day a coffee at one of the many open-air harbourside cafés is excellent, but such is the throng you may be lucky to find a seat. Nyhavn's restaurants are also worth considering. Though not the best that Copenhagen has to offer (and not the cheapest either), they are among the most atmospheric, whether you eat inside or, in the summer, outside beside the harbour. Nyhavn also has one of the city's most delightful hotels, No. 71, created from an old warehouse. During the last weeks before Christmas the outdoor cafés of Nyhavn are replaced by stalls selling gifts and decorations which make risking the chill wind that can sweep up the harbour worthwhile.

At the city end of Nyhavn the huge anchor is a memorial to the Danish seamen who died in World War II serving in the Allied merchant navies. Beyond is **Kongens Nytorv**, the King's new square, the King in

THE REJECTED LIBRARIAN

Fed up with the rigours of writing and the uncertainties of book sales, in 1834 Hans Christian Andersen applied for a job at the Royal Library. The authorities were unimpressed and rejected his application. Andersen did not write a fable about a rejected librarian, which is sad as it might have redressed the balance, his application now being one of the Library's treasured possessions.

question being Christian V whose statue adorns it. The square was once more intimate, the intimacy created by numerous trees which have succumbed to Dutch elm disease and road 'improvements'. The tree-shorn square may be easier for traffic to negotiate, but is now bare, weatherswept and, though impressive, rather impersonal. On the square's southern side is **Det Kongelige Teater**, the Royal Theatre, built in 1872. It is actually two theatres in one and is the city's centre for ballet and opera as well as plays. Beside it is **Charlottenborg**, built in Baroque style in 1643 as a royal palace and now the home of the Royal Academy of Fine Arts, with a frequently changing programme of exhibitions of contemporary art (open daily 10:00–17:00, but Wed until 19:00). The western side of the square is dominated by the very grand **Hotel d'Angleterre**. Close to it (on the corner of Strøget) is the **Magasin du Nord**, which was Denmark's first departmental store. The name derives from the Hotel du Nord which formerly stood on the site. On the far, opposite corner the **Ravhuset** sells jewellery made from Baltic

KING CHRISTIAN V

The equestrian statue of King Christian V which now stands in Kongens Nytorv is a 1946 bronze replica of the original which, as it had been cast in lead, in 1688, was so heavy that the king gradually collapsed his poor horse.

Below: *Nyhavn is one of the most picturesque spots in Copenhagen (or in any European city).*

CHANGING THE GUARD

When Queen Margrethe is in residence at Amalienborg – look for the royal standard – the guard is changed daily at 12:00. The new guard leaves the Rosenborg Slot at 11:30 and marches along Gothersgade, Frederiksborgade, Købmagergade, Østergade, Kongens Nytorv and Bredgade to reach the Marmorkirken and Amalienborg Slot. The changeover is accomplished with great dignity, and members of the public who do not share this view – perhaps by sitting or appearing to jest at the proceedings – are given an official dressing down by zealous officials.

amber and has a small amber museum (open May–Sept daily 10:00–19:30; Oct–April 10:00–17:30 in winter).

FREDERIKSSTADEN ★

North of Nyhavn lies **Frederiksstaden**, the brainchild of King Frederik V who wanted to celebrate 300 years of the House of Oldbenburg with a grand building project. Frederik donated the land, but the buildings were mostly funded by the Danish aristocracy and rich merchants, these gentlemen apparently deciding that they could not afford not to be involved. The new area was laid out on a grand scale – visitors arriving from Nyhavn will think that with a dozen steps they have been transported from Copenhagen to Paris – and much of the work was done to designs by Nicolai Eigtved. To see the best of this grand architecture, take **Bredgade** which leaves Kongens Nytorv from the top end of Nyhavn. Bredgade as well as the streets which leave it are favoured by Copenhagen's professionals, solicitors and the like, and also antique dealers.

At a crossroads about halfway along, the **Amalienborg Slot** lies to the right. The palace has been the home of the Danish royal family since 1794 when fire destroyed Christiansborg, but was originally four separate mansions built around an airy cobbled square. At the centre of the square is a huge equestrian statue of Frederik V (depicted as a Roman Emperor by the French sculptor Jacques Saly). The statue took 20 years to complete , but this had less to do with its complexity than the problems of funding. The northernmost palace (the Levetzau Palace) is open to the public, and visitors can enjoy the splendid rooms and the often startling collections of former royal residents (open May–Oct daily 10:00–16:00; Nov–

Apr Tue–Sun 11:00–16:00).

Walking through Amalienborg Plads and then on between the palaces on its southeastern side the visitor reaches Amaliehaven, a waterside park. Turn left here for a quiet walk to **Den Kongelige Afstøbningssamlingen**, the Royal Cast Collection, with several thousand plaster casts of sculptures covering 4000 years of world art (open Wed 14:00–20:00, Sun 14:00–17:00). To add further spice to the walk, it is not uncommon to meet the Queen, Prince Henrik or both walking the royal dachshunds beside the harbour.

On Bredgade opposite the turn to the palace is the **Marmorkirken**, the Marble Church, more correctly called Frederikskirken. Begun in 1749 to a design by Eigtved, work was stopped in 1770 by Count von Struensee (doctor to King Christian VII and lover of his queen – see

Above: *Frederikskirken, better known by all city dwellers as Marmorkirken, the Marble Church.*
Opposite: *Wrapped up against the chill of winter a guard watches over the Amalienborg Slot.*

panel, page 20) when expenditure started to get out of hand. By the time work started again about a century later, the 10m (33ft) walls had become a grass-covered mound. The walls were unearthed and the church was completed in Danish limestone rather than the planned Norwegian marble, though the colloquial name stuck. With its huge dome, modelled on St Peter's in the Vatican, the church is one of Copenhagen's most dominant landmarks (open Mon, Tue and Thu 10:00–17:00, Wed 10:00–18:00, Fri–Sun 12:00–17:00). The dome also dominates the interior, though the royal box pew and the paintings of the Apostles are worth seeking out. Outside, the church is ringed by statues of the great and the good of Danish history (these include Kierkegaard, an irony in view of his long-standing philosophical battle with the

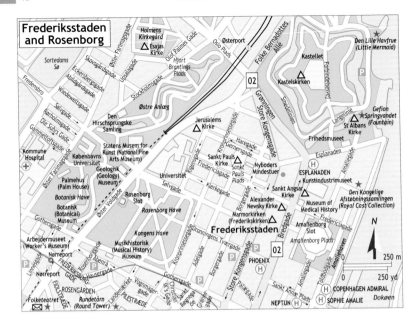

Frederiksstaden and Rosenborg

Map labels: Sortedams Sø, Øster Farimagsgade, Skovgårdsgade, Uralagade, Holmens Kirkegård, Esajas Kirke, Olof Palmes Gade, Hjort Brantings Plads, Østerport, Oslo Plads, Folke Bernadottes Allé, Kastellet, Den Lille Havfrue (Little Mermaid), Fortinindelsesvej, Kastelskirken, Eckersbergsgade, Abildgårdsgade, Wiedeweltsgade, Fredensbro, Stockholmsgade, Østre Anlæg, Sølvgade, Rørholmsgade, Ole Suhrs Gade, Gammeltoftsgade, Den Hirschsprungske Samling, Jerusalems Kirke, Grønningen, Store Kongensgade, Gefion Springvandet (Fountain), Langelinie, St Albans Kirke, Frihedsmuseet, Kommune Hospital, Øster Farimagsgade, Københavns Universitet, Statens Museum for Kunst (National Fine Arts Museum), Geologisk (Geology) Museum, Haregade, Gernersgade, Sankt Pauls Kirke, Fredericiagade, Sankt Pauls Plads, Nyboders Mindestuer, Esplanaden, ESPLANADEN, Kunstindustrimuseet, Palmehus (Palm House), Universitet, Sølvgade, Klerkegade, Sankt Ansgar Kirke, Den Kongelige Afstøbningssamlingen (Royal Cast Collection), Botanisk Have, Rosenborg Slot, Alexander Newsky Kirke, Museum of Medical History, Botanisk (Botanical) Museum, Gothersgade, Øster Voldgade, Rosenborg Have, Marmorkirken (Frederikskirken), Amalienborg Slot, Kongens Have, Frederiksstaden, Amalienborg Plads, Arbejdermuseet (Worker's Museum), Nørreport, Musikhistorisk (Musical History) Museum, Rosenborggade, Åbenrå, Dronningens Tværgade, Kronprinsessegade, Adelgade, Borgergade, Store Kongensgade, PHOENIX, Amaliegade, Toldbodgade, Amalienhaven, N, 250 m, 250 yd, Nørreport, FREDERIKSBORG, Hauser gade, Linnésgade, Vognmagergade, Gothersgade, Christian IX's Gade, Sankt Christian, Regnegade, Grønnegade, Pilestræde, Landemærket, Palægade, Sankt Annæ Plads, COPENHAGEN ADMIRAL, Folketeatret, Rundetårn (Round Tower), NEPTUN, SOPHIE AMALIE, Dokøen

Opposite: *The equestrian statue of Frederik V dominates the centre of the Amalienborg Plads.*

church which, many contend, resulted in his early death).

Next along Bredgade is **Alexander Newsky Kirke**, a church built, appropriately, in Russian Byzantine style, complete with golden onion domes, in 1881. Princess Dagmar, daughter of Danish King Christian IX, married the man who became Czar Alexander III and converted to the Russian Orthodox church. The church was built by her for the Russian Orthodox congregation in Copenhagen. Alexander Newsky was a 13th-century Russian prince and warrior who was later made a saint. The church is only open during services.

Opposite the church is a **Museum of Medical History**, housed in what was once a hospital, then the home of the Royal Academy of Surgeons. The collection covers everything from the informative through the bizarre to the disgusting – something for everyone, really (guided tours in English Jul–Aug, Wed–Fri at 11:00 and 13:00 and Sun at 13:00). Next to the museum is **Sankt Ansgar Kirke**, Copenhagen's Catholic Cathedral – a small building in charming neo-Romanesque style. The cathedral has a small collection of Danish Catholicism (view by appointment only). Next again is the **Kunstindustrimuseet**, a fascinating museum on the history of decorative and applied art. The museum has a vast collection covering the last 400 years or so of domestic design, with rooms furnished in period styles (open Tue–Sun 12:00–16:00).

Ahead now is parkland surrounding the Kastellet, but if time permits turn left along Esplanaden, then follow Gernersgade into **Nyboder**, an area of quaint streets the houses of which were home to navy seamen in 18th-century Copenhagen. The **Nyboders Mindestuer** is a museum exploring the area's history (open all year, Wed at 11:00–14:00 and Sun at 11:00–16:00). Close by, **Sankt Pauls Kirke** stands in a beautiful timeless square.

Alternatively, turn east along Esplanaden, passing, to the left, the **Frihedsmuseet** dedicated to the Danish resistance during the later stages of World War II, when Germany finally imposed military governorship on occupied Denmark (open May to Sep Tue–Sat 10:00–16:00, Sun 10:00–17:00; Oct to Apr Tue–Sat 10:00–15:00, Sun 10:00–16:00). At the far end of the museum, turn left along **Langelinie**, a walkway between the sea and Kastellet, one famous for its sculptures and one to which

> **AMBER MUSEUM**
>
> The upper floor of the shop at Kongens Nytorv 2 is a small museum of amber. Much of the world's supply of amber (fossilized tree resin) comes from the Baltic, the museum having pieces of various colours, some with trapped insects, and one of the largest chunks ever discovered. There are also amber chess sets, etc.

> **THE LEGEND OF GEFION**
>
> In Norse mythology it is said that the King of Sweden offered the goddess Gefion as much land as she could plough in one night. Gefion changed her four sons into massive oxen and used them to plough the whole of Zealand, removing the island from the Swedish crown.

The Little Mermaid had her head removed in the 1960s and an arm sawn off in the 1980s, neither item ever being recovered – a recasting and grafting were required to return her to completeness. She lost her head again in 1998, but this time it was found a few days later in a cardboard box outside a television studio. No one has ever been charged for these amputations, the unkind suggesting a long list of suspects as the world is full of art lovers.

Below: *The Gefion Fountain, a masterwork by Anders Bundgaard which is too often over-looked by visitors heading for the Little Mermaid.*

all visitors gravitate. On the left is **St Albans Kirke**, Copenhagen's Anglican church in pure English Gothic style. Next is the **Gefion Fountain**, one of the city's artistic masterpieces. It took sculptor Anders Bundgaard eleven years to sculpt his vision of the Gefion myth.

Beyond the fountain is a delightful seaside stroll – occasionally enlivened by a passing cruise ship – and several other thought-provoking works of art before the statue for which Copenhagen has become famous, **Den Lille Havfrue**, the Little Mermaid, is reached. The statue was funded by Carl Jacobsen, the Carlsberg beer magnate, who was inspired by a ballet itself inspired by Hans Christian Andersen's tale of a mermaid who falls in love with a human prince. The statue was the work of Edvard Eriksen in the 1910s. Eriksen modelled the face on the ballerina Ellen Price, the body on his wife Eline. Visitors trek to this remote place beside the sea to see, photograph and be photographed beside the Little Mermaid. Yet for all its fame the statue is disappointing – small, somewhat uninspiring and positioned against an industrial backdrop across the water. In fairness, few of the world's renowned sights measure up to the anticipation heaped on them by the eager visitor.

Continue along Langelinie, which bears left away from the Little Mermaid and the sea, then turn left to cross the moat of the **Kastellet**. This vast and impressively defended fortress was King Frederik III's response (in 1662) to the Swedish siege of 1658, though it utilized the foundations of earlier defences. The surrounding moat (in places still a double moat) is shaped as a five-pointed star, the track around the ramparts inside it now a favourite walking/jogging

track for city folk. On the King's Bastion (on the western side) there is a marvellous windmill. The buildings within the defences were once the barracks of the Danish army. Some troops are still housed here in the delightful terraced houses – even in so functional a building the Danes still exhibit great style. One part of the building houses a small museum of army uniforms, etc. (Kastellet open all year, daily at 06:00–22:00; Museum May–Sept, Sun 12:00–16:00). Further north, near Hellerup, the Experimentarium is a new science and technology based centre which both children and adults will enjoy. Open Mon, Wed, Fri 9:30–17:00, Tue 9:30–21:00, Sat and Sun 11:00–17:00.

ROSENBORG **

To the west of the Kastellet lies a beautiful swathe of parkland that offers a tranquil option to the bustle of central Copenhagen as well as acting as the city's lungs. **Østre Anlæg** is the most northerly section of the park, a marvellous place where trees, shrubs, flowers and lakes combine to telling effect. Within it stands the **Statens Museum for Kunst**, the National Fine Arts Museum, its older building by Vilhelm Dahlerup, the new extension opened in 1990 (open Tue, Thu–Sun 10:00–17:00, Wed 10:00–20:00).

Above: *The Little Mermaid draws a regular stream of visitors who come to photograph it or be photographed with it.*

STRUENSEE'S DEATH

After his arrest Count Struensee, doctor to King Christian VII and lover of his queen (see panel, page 20), was imprisoned in the Kastellet. As Struensee had the King's permission to enact the policies which so enraged the aristocracy he was not actually guilty of any crime, and so was convicted of his adultery with Queen Caroline Matilda. His right hand (the one that signed the hated decrees) was chopped off, followed quickly by his head. His body was then quartered and put on public display.

Above: *Kongens Have, part of the lovely parkland beside Rosenborg Slot.*
Opposite: *The Golden Crown is considered the richest treasure among the Danish Crown Jewels.*

The museum has an inspiring collection of Danish art, as well as works by Rubens, Brueghel, Matisse and Picasso.

Across the lake behind the art museum is a second museum, **Den Hirschsprungske Samling**, the donated collection of a tobacco magnate, which concentrates on 19th- and 20th-century Danish art (open daily, except Tue, 11:00–16:00).

The southerly park is **Botanisk Have**. This, too, has a lake at its heart around which are planted species chiefly from northern Europe. At the northeastern corner is a small **Geology Museum** with a collection illustrating Danish and Greenlandic geology (open Tue–Sun 13:00–16:00). The museum houses a 20-ton meteorite, one of the largest ever found – shades of *Miss Smilla's Feeling for Snow* (see panel, page 55). There is also a **Botanical Museum** which concentrates on plant life of the same two countries (open Jun–Aug daily 12:00–16:00). This museum lies at the other end of the park, and the visitor is treated to a fine walk between the two, a walk which takes in a palm house if the western side of the lake is followed. Cross Gothersgade from the Botanical Museum, then turn right into Rømersgade to reach the **Arbejdermuseet**, the Worker's Museum. Behind a bust of Lenin this distinctly left-leaning museum explores the often poor and unjust history of the ordinary Dane. It is frequently filled with schoolchildren, a sign of the health of Danish democracy (open all year daily 10:00–16:00).

CL DAVIDS SAMLING

Close to Kongens Have is the collection of Islamic and European art of the barrister Christian David who died in 1960. The European artwork is interesting but hardly breathtaking; however, the Islamic art most certainly is. David accumulated the finest collection of its type in Scandinavia, with superb texts, ceramics, glass, silver and textiles dating from the 8th century (open Tue, Thu–Sun 13:00–16:00, Wed 10:00–16:00).

Turning left along Gothersgade the visitor passes, on the right, the **Musical History Museum** (open May–Sep Fri–Wed 13:00–15:50; Oct–Apr Mon, Wed, Sat, Sun 13:00–15:50) to reach, on the left, the entrance to **Kongens Have** and **Rosenborg Have**, twin gardens set beside the Rosenborg Slot. The gardens were laid out, to a design by King Christian IV, at the time the castle was being built and are a delight, a mix of the formal, with trimmed hedges and roses in rows, and the natural. A puppet theatre plays here on most afternoons in summer, the free show enjoyed by picnickers. The moated **Rosenborg Slot** beside the gardens is the most picturesque of Copenhagen's royal palaces, built by Christian IV as a summer house, but later extended to become his main residence. After Frederik IV moved to Fredensborg, the royal family opened Rosenborg (entrance in Øster Voldgade, not from the gardens) to display the eclectic collection that the magpie-like Christian IV had accumulated during his long reign. Rosenborg also beautifully portrays the life of the king and his successors, sparing no detail: King Christian's writing desk is here, but so too is his toilet, elegantly covered in blue tiling – style as well as function, the essence of Danish design (open May and Sep daily 10:00–16:00, Jun–Aug daily 10:00–17:00, Oct daily 10:00–16:00, Jan–Apr Tue–Sun 11:00–14:00).

CHRISTIANSHAVN *

Across the water from central Copenhagen, set on the northern end of the island of Amager, is **Christianshavn**. This area was created, under orders from King Christian IV, as a commercial centre (the canals were cut to increase the wharfing areas for shipping) and as a buffer zone (invading armies needed to capture it on their way to the city). The King's original idea was for much more elaborate and complex defences, but this was reduced because of burgeoning costs.

THE CROWN JEWELS

The highlight of a tour of Rosenborg Slot is the collection of Danish crown jewels. The Golden Crown of Absolute Monarchy is studded with diamonds, rubies and sapphires, while Christian III's jewel-encrusted sword is equally impressive. So remarkable is the collection that Queen Margrethe is not allowed to take many of the items abroad when she travels.

MUSIKHISTORISK MUSEUM OG CARL CLAUDIUS' SAMLING

The music history museum (and Claudius collection) has a virtually complete set of musical instruments from Europe, Africa and Asia spanning the history of music making across the centuries. There is also a collection of curios that will intrigue music lovers of all tastes.

WRONG THREAD?

The ascent of the spire of Vor Frelsers Kirke starts with an indoor expedition through the church's roofing timbers and ends with an increasingly tight and vertigo-inducing external climb. An early ascent was that of King Frederick V who received the cheers of the crowd and a 27-gun salute when he reached the top. The stairway was the work of Laurids de Thurah, but there is no truth in the often-told tale that he threw himself from the top when he realized the builders had made the stairway spiral the wrong way.

Opposite: *The distinctively spiraled spire of Vor Frelsers Kirke in Christianshavn.*

Though neither as picturesque as the main city, nor having as many sights, Christianshavn is still worth a visit, especially in the early morning to catch the swarms of cyclists on Knippelsbro.

Across the bridge, a right turn into Strandgade takes you to the **Burmeister & Wein Museet**, which explores the history of the diesel engine. The curious title is from a local company which pioneered marine diesel engines. During World War II the B&W factory in Christianshavn made U-boat engines and was bombed by the British (open daily 10:00–13:00). Further on is **Christianskirke**, built in rococo style to a design by Nicolai Eigtved who died a few years before its completion. The church was built for Christianshavn's German community and was paid for by a lottery, giving it the still-heard name of Lottery Church. Inside, the church is laid out in a unique theatre-like manner.

Go back along Strandgade and you'll reach the **Arkitekcentret**, housed in the converted warehouses of Gammel Dok, where temporary exhibitions explore some aspects of Denmark's architectural heritage. Arguably the finest exhibit of all is the beautifully restored warehousing itself. From Gammel Dok a waterway can be followed to **Christianshavn Kanal**, the main canal. Though not as pretty as Nyhavn, the canal has great character and is well worth strolling along. On its southern side is the **Orlogsmuseet**, the Royal Danish Naval Museum, which explores the navy's history with a terrific collection of model ships and other memorabilia. There are models of famous sea battles and a replica submarine which children will love. They'll love the playroom too (open Tue–Sun 12:00–16:00).

Christianshavn

Near the museum is the unmistakable **Vor Frelsers Kirke** (Church of Our Saviour), with its copper and gold spire up which a staircase spirals. The church, built in the last years of the 17th century, has a very rich interior with fine carvings and an organ of 4000 pipes. It is possible to climb the spire, from the top of which there is a great view of Christianshavn and towards the city.

From Vor Frelsers Kirke it is a short walk to the free state of **Christiania** (*see* panel, page 23), which is well worth a visit. Despite its dubious image the free state has some very good eateries and cafés, an interesting exhibition on renewable energy sources and alternative living, and a concert hall that hosts world-famous rock artists.

Close to Christiania is **Lille Mølle**, the Little Windmill, set on the ramparts of Christianshavn. The mill was built in 1669 and was converted to a private house in the early 20th century.

Its interior has been preserved and now forms part of the National Museum. From the mill it is possible to gain an idea of the fortifications of Christianshavn which made it a crucial outer defence of Copenhagen, the ramparts linking a series of bastions which thrust belligerently in the direction of a probable invasion.

VESTERBRO ★

The vast majority of the best sights that Copenhagen has to offer lie to the east of Tivoli, but heading west from Central Station is worthwhile to catch a couple of the city's more unusual offerings. Whether you view the attractions on **Istedgade** as interesting, light-hearted or disgusting depends on your viewpoint on the more in-

---

MISS SMILLA JASPERSEN

Christianshavn is the home of Smilla Jaspersen, the Greenlander hero of Peter Høeg's novel *Miss Smilla's Feeling for Snow*, and it is there that the death of a boy leads her into a story that is part thriller, part philosophy. The book, which won wide critical acclaim, has recently been made into a film which unaccountably shortened the book's title and missed much of its subtlety.

Right: *One of the many murals which enliven the walls of the 'free city' of Christiania.*

ØKSNEHALLEN

Though in general no longer the avant-garde area it was, Copenhagen southwest of the Central Station still makes its contribution. Head south from Istedgade to Øksnehallen where an old industrial site has been turned into an exhibition centre for art and culture.

CARLSBERG

Christen Jacobsen (1773–1835) learned his trade as a brewer at the King's Brewery on Slotsholmen, passing his knowledge to his son Jacob Christian Jacobsen (1811–87) who toured Germany to discover a recipe for a better beer than the barely drinkable Danish beers of the time. Jacob built his own brewery on a hill to the west of the city, naming it for his son Carl – Carl's Hill, Carlsberg. Carl Jacobsen (1842–1914) fell out with his father and built his own brewery, but he shared Jacob's philanthropic zeal. Jacob had endowed scientific and historic centres, whereas Carl preferred the arts, the Glyptotek being the most striking affirmation.

your-face Danish liberalism. This is the capital's centre for sex shops and strip clubs, but what was once shocking and avant-garde now seems mostly seedy.

At the edge of the Sankt Jørgens Sø basin stands the futuristic **Tycho Brahe Planetarium** (*see* panel, page 42). The planetarium has a vast dome-shaped screen on which the latest technology allows shows of all things heavenly, including the northern lights. The screen is also used for Omnimax films (open Mon–Fri 09:30–21:00, Sat–Sun 10:30–21:00). Nearby, on Vesterbrogade, the **Københavns Bymuseet** (Copenhagen City Museum) explores the history and development of the city from Bishop Absalon's time to the present. The model of 17th-century Copenhagen is staggering – the city has grown amazingly in three centuries. The museum also has a small collection of Kierkegaard memorabilia including some unpleasant period cartoons that exaggerated his spinal deformity (open all year Mon and Thurs–Sun 10:00–16:00, Wed 10:00–21:00).

Further on – buses 8 and 28 from Rådhuspladsen can be used – the visitor will find the Carlsberg Brewery and Frederiksberg, a separate township despite being a suburb of the city. The **Bakkehusmuseet**, standing in the shadow of the brewery, is a collection of memorabilia of Denmark's own Renaissance (1775–1825) housed in a 17th-century house (open Wed, Thu, Sat, Sun 11:00–15:00). The brewery's most famous feature is the Elephant Gate, as improbable an entranceway as you will ever see, which is on a public road. The brewery has a visitors centre, with exhibits on its history (open Tue–Sun 10:00–16:00) which includes a museum displaying a historical overview of brewing.

From the Carlsberg site it is a short walk to **Frederiksberg Have**, a large park in English style which, in spring when the bulbs and flowers bloom, is one of Copenhagen's most beautiful open spaces. On the west side of the park is the city's **zoo** (open daily 09:00–17:00, until 18:00 in summer) with the usual collection of species. There is a children's zoo and a huge tower from which the city and Sweden can be seen. Dominating the park is **Frederiksberg Slot**, built by Frederik IV in the early 18th century as a summer residence. It is open to the public on very few occasions when guided tours are organized. Tours can also be made of the **Royal Copenhagen Porcelain Factory** at the other end of the park (tours Mon–Fri at 09:00, 10:00, 11:00, 13:00, 14:00). Even those shocked by the price of the Flora Danica, claimed (with justification) to be the world's most expensive dinner service, will be interested in the production and hand-painting process. The Circus Museum at Hvidovre, south-east of the city centre (Bus 133) which has Europe's biggest collection of artefacts and where children can dress up and try their hand at juggling etc. Open Mon, Tue and Sun 11:00–15:00.

Below: *The famous Elephant Gate at the Carlsberg Brewery. Strangely the gate actually stands astride a public road.*

Copenhagen at a Glance

Most people visit in summer and, with the city's best sites being within walking distance of each other, warm days are a bonus for exploration. The city has good parks and spring, when the bulbs bloom, and autumn, when the leaves turn colour, are picturesque. Winter can be exhilarating, but can also be very cold.

Most visitors to Copenhagen arrive by plane at Kastrup Airport, a terrific new airport west of the city centre. From it trains, buses and taxis reach the city centre in 15–20 minutes. The best transport is the S-train, the service running from beneath the airport entrance with trains every 20 minutes. The Central Station (København H) is the third stop, after Tårnby and Ørestad. Motorists will find a motorway (E20) just outside the airport. Follow this and signs for City Centre to arrive at the Central Station. The motorway goes over the new Øresund bridge and so can be used if arriving from Sweden. Copenhagen's Central Station is reached by trains from Germany (and the rest of Europe) and Scandinavia. The city is also a ferry port for travellers from the UK, Scandinavia, and Poland.

Copenhagen has excellent metro and bus systems. The metro (S-train) has 10 lines all of which intersect at Central Station (København H), Vesterport, Nørreport and Østerport. The system runs as far as Helsingør (north), Køge (south) and Roskilde and Frederikssund (west). To the east the S-train links the city to the airport and, via the Øresund link, with Malmö. The bus system – HT buses – are efficient and operate to and through the central bus station in Rådhuspladsen. The two systems use the same tickets. Discount tickets are available. The Copenhagen Card gives visitors unlimited travel on the systems as well as free admission to most museums and galleries (including the Tivoli).

A range of accommodation is available in Copenhagen. The Tourist Information Office has a list and offers assistance.

LUXURY

Radisson SAS Royal Hotel, Hammerischsgade 1, 1611 Copenhagen V, tel: 33 426000, fax: 33 426100. Tower block designed by Arne Jacobsen and built in 1960. Opposite the Tivoli, central position, every comfort. Past guests include Tina Turner and the Dalai Lama; 265 rooms.

Hotel d'Angleterre, Kongens Nytorv 34, 1050 Copenhagen K, tel: 33 120095, fax: 33 121118. Old-fashioned grace, elegance and levels of service.

Midway between the Tivoli and Amalienborg, palace-facing in outlook; 124 rooms.

Radisson SAS Scandinavia Hotel, Amager Boulevard 70, 2300 Copenhagen S, tel: 33 965000, fax: 33 965500. Near the airport and the E20. Modern and huge, but not impersonal; 542 rooms.

MID-RANGE

Copenhagen Triton Hotel, Helgolandsgade 7/11, 1653 Copenhagen V, tel: 33 313266, fax: 33 316970. Near the Central Station and the Tivoli. Slightly faded, but still good value; 123 rooms.

71 Nyhavn, Nyhavn 71, 1051 Copenhagen K, tel: 33 436200, fax: 33 436201. At the expensive end of the range, but one of the most charming hotels in the city. A converted 200-year warehouse on Nyhavn itself; 82 rooms.

Hotel City, Peder Skrams Gade 24, 1054 Copenhagen K, tel: 33 130666, fax: 33 130667. Between Nyhavn and the sea, so a short walk from the city. Small Best Western, quiet and comfortable; 81 rooms.

BUDGET

Hotel Selandia, Helgolandsgade 12, 1653 Copenhagen V, tel: 33 314610, fax: 33 314609. Inexpensive, but very friendly. Near Tivoli and the Central Station, 84 rooms.

Hotel Jørgensen, Rømersgade 11, 1362 Copenhagen K, tel: 33 138186, fax: 33 155105.

Copenhagen at a Glance

Near the Nørreport S-train station. Has both rooms and dormitories. Popular with gay travellers, but open to all.

Cab-Inn Scandinavia, Vodroffsvei 55, 1900 Frederiksberg C, tel: 35 361111, fax: 35 361114. Modern, with compact rooms like cruise-ship cabins (hence the name). Excellent for those who don't mind travelling a bit to reach the city and save money as a result; 201 rooms.

WHERE TO EAT

Copenhagen has plenty of restaurants and the Tourist Office has a guide to them so you can decide between traditional Danish cooking or a kangaroo steak at the Reef 'n' Beef, an Australian restaurant in Jarmers Plads. Tivoli has a range that varies from a burger to the stylish Divan 2 and the Nimb. Recommended are:

Copenhagen Corner, Vesterbrogade 1, 1620 Copenhagen K, tel: 33 914545, fax: 33 910404. Next to the shopping gallery across the street from the Rådhuspladsen. Danish menu with a hint of French. Terrific ambience, great views from window tables. Expensive.

Frascati, Vesterbrogade 9A, 1620 Copenhagen K, tel: 33 156690, fax: 33 910150. First-class Italian restaurant just beyond the Central Station. Nicely decorated. Excellent service. Moderately expensive.

SARS Kommandøren, Nyhavn 15, 1051 Copenhagen K, tel: 33 145614. One of the best Nyhavn restaurants. Particularly good at lunchtime when the soup and smørrebrød are excellent. Moderately expensive.

SHOPPING

Strøget offers the best shopping in Copenhagen, ranging from internationally famous names and such Danish names as Royal Copenhagen, incorporating Georg Jensen, Bang & Olufsen, and Holmegaard, the Zealand glassware company. Illums Bolighus and Magasin du Nord, two departmental stores, are also in this street. Some up-and-coming names of Danish fashion are either in Strøget or in the streets that lead off it. For particular types of shops, get a copy of the Copenhagen shopping guide, published by the Tourist Office. There are good flea markets: in Gammel Strand on Sat and Sun mornings for antiques and superior bric-a-brac; in Israel Plads on Sat mornings for just about everything, and in Smallegade, Frederiksberg on Sat mornings, also for anything you can think of.

TOURS AND EXCURSIONS

The Tourist Information Office has details of tours of the city and excursions to Zealand (and further afield). Consider a canal boat tour to get a new angle on the city sights, or a bus tour. An excellent (free) walking tour is the Nightwatchman Tour every night Jun–Aug at 21:00. It starts at Gråbrødre Torv – just turn up and follow the man in the strange costume carrying a big mace for an hour of fun and information with a slightly off-beat theme.

USEFUL CONTACTS

Wonderful Copenhagen Tourist Information Office, Bernstorffsgade 1 (near the Central Station and Tivoli main entrance, and the Hard Rock Café), tel: 70 222442, issues a *Copenhagen This Week* brochure with news of events and opening times.

Use It, Rådhusstræde 13, tel: 33 730620. Aimed at budget travellers, but useful for all.

Danish Tourist Board, Vesterbrogade 6D, tel: 33 111415, has information about places outside the city.

News in English is broadcast Mon–Fri at 08:30, 17.05 and 22:00 on 1062kHz.

COPENHAGEN	J	F	M	A	M	J	J	A	S	O	N	D
AVERAGE TEMP. °C	0	0	2	7	12	16	18	17	14	9	5	3
AVERAGE TEMP. °F	32	32	36	45	54	61	64	63	57	48	41	37
RAINFALL mm	49	39	32	38	40	47	71	66	62	59	48	49
RAINFALL in	1.9	1.5	1.3	1.5	1.6	1.9	2.8	2.6	2.4	2.3	1.9	1.9

3
North Jutland

Though it is by far the largest part of Denmark, dwarfing Zealand, Jutland is the least known. Visitors do come, some drawn by the delights of **Legoland**, others by the scenic beauty of the lakes around **Silkeborg** or the glimpse of Denmark's Viking past at **Jelling** and **Ribe**. Some get no further than Copenhagen or, perhaps, a day trip to Odense if it is Hans Christian Andersen they seek. But to ignore Jutland is to miss out. Not only are there important historical sites – Tollund Man is one of the wonders of ancient Europe – but beautiful scenery, particularly along the coast where the dune systems are a highlight, but also inland where ancient heathland and woodlands still flourish. In **Aalborg** and **Århus** Jutland boasts Denmark's third and fourth biggest towns, each with its own story, and it also has a multitude of fascinating villages. Not so long ago Jutland was remote from Copenhagen and difficult to reach. But the construction of the bridge between Zealand and Fyn, and the motorway system which links Fyn to Jutland, and then crosses Jutland from east to west and north to south, allow visitors to reach Århus and Aalborg easily. Buses go from Copenhagen to Århus in three hours, to Aalborg in five. There are regular flights to the two cities so visitors can fly to Jutland, explore its delights by car and then drive back to Copenhagen. A flight to Aalborg is a fine introduction to Jutland. After crossing the coastline the plane descends over a patchwork of fields and past the clustered houses of little villages, with an expanse of water gleaming in the distance. A county to delight the senses.

Don't Miss

*** **Silkeborg:** beautiful country and Tollund Man.
*** **Aalborg:** a lovely little town, and a superb base for exploring.
*** **Den Gamle By:** Denmark's best open-air museum, at Århus.
** **Råbjerg Mile:** fantastic dune systems and seascapes.
** **Rebild Bakker:** national park with forest trails.
* **Fyrkat:** reconstructed Viking fort.
* **Lindholm Høje:** atmospheric Viking burial site.

Opposite: *Maren Turis Gade, one of the prettiest places in Aalborg.*

Opposite: *CW Obels Plads, the delightful square at the heart of Aalborg.*

AALBORG ★★★

Limfjorden cuts right across northern Jutland, separating the northern tip from the rest of the jutting peninsula. At the point where Limfjorden is narrowest stands **Aalborg**, placed to take advantage of the narrowing, and of the sheltered access to the sea that Limfjorden offers. The Vikings realized the strategic significance of the position, their town flourishing as a trading and herring-fishing port. The **shipbuilding** that formed part of the commerce of a Viking port also laid the foundation of Aalborg's later prosperity, and the trade is still an employer today, though the major construction required by today's markets is not feasible in the narrow Limfjorden. Aalborg is also famous as a centre for the production of **akvavit**, the Danish version of schnapps, as those who try the drink in any part of Denmark will rapidly realize by studying the bottle label. Today the thriving town also has its own university and symphony orchestra.

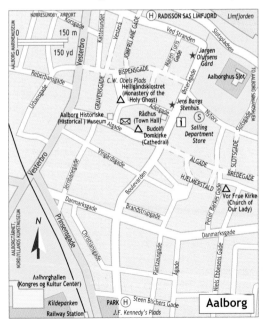

Modern Aalborg occupies both sides of Limfjorden though it is not always advisable to say so to a resident of **Nørresundby** which was 'officially united', or 'consumed', depending upon your point of view, with Aalborg in 1970. The original town grew up on the fjord's southern bank and that is where the major places of interest lie. To explore the city, start at **CW Obels Plads**, a delightful square where visitors can enjoy a cup of coffee at the outdoor tables. The **Monastery of the Holy Ghost** on the square is the oldest old people's home in Denmark, founded in 1431 and made a monastery by Papal decree in 1451. It has good 16th-century frescoes. To the west of the square is Aalborg's **Historical Museum** with a good history of the city and exquisite wall panelling (open Tue–Sun 10:00–17:00). South of the square, the **Town Hall** is a beautiful Baroque building, while opposite it,

Jens Bangs Stenhus is considered by many to be the finest merchant's house in northern Europe. It was built in 1624. On the other side of CW Obels Plads, in Maren Turis Gade, is **Jørgen Olufsens Gård**, a picturesque collection of 17th-century half-timbered merchants' houses.

Close to the town hall is the **cathedral**, built in the early 15th century and dedicated to the English St Botolph, the patron saint of sailors. Inside there is a superb Baroque altar and a portrait of Caroline Matilda, wife of Christian VII and lover of Count Struensee (*see* panel, page 20). Another fine church can be found in the pedestrianized area to the southeast of CW Obels Plads. **Vor Frue Kirke** (Church of Our Lady) dates from the 12th century, but was rebuilt in the 15th. It stands at the heart of some very picturesque streets, and to the south of **Aalborghus Slot**, which was built in the mid-16th century to house the king's tax collector who presumably needed the protection of stout walls. The castle is now the administrative centre of north Jutland.

Finally, two other curiosities are worth visiting if time permits. **Greenland House**, in the southern city, has an amazing collection of Inuit art and artefacts, while the **Aalborgtårnet** is a spidery tower from which there is a fine view of the city. There is also a good café at the top. After descending the tower, the nearby **Nordjyllands Kunstmuseum** (Museum of Modern and Contemporary Art) is worth visiting for its collection of 20th-century

A POINTED OPINION

The rich decoration of his house indicates the wealth of Jens Bang. But despite his social standing he was declined a place on the Town Council. His view of the decision is reflected in one carved face on the side of the house facing the Town Hall. The face's tongue is poked out towards the Hall.

AALBORG OR ÅLBORG?

In 1948 the Danes decided to adopt the letter 'å' used in other Scandinavian countries, replacing the 'aa' previously used. Many places, like Århus in Jutland, changed immediately, but some, notably Aalborg, decided to stay with what they were used to. The 'å' has two sounds: either 'aw' or 'o'. In Aalborg's case the 'aa' takes the former, making the name 'Awlborg'.

painting by Danish and
foreign artists (open Tue–Sun
10:00–17:00.

THE VERY NORTH ★★

To the north of Nørresundby
lies **Lindholm Høje**, Denmark's largest Viking burial
ground. The site has about
700 graves, most of them
cremations enclosed by
ship-shaped lines of stones.
The site museum has many
of the grave goods from the
site, most of them personal items which makes them
all the more moving. The site was the cemetery of a
nearby village, one Viking field having been preserved,
a unique feature (site open at all times; museum
open Apr–Oct Tues 10:00–15:00, Nov–Mar Sun
11:00–16:00).

The E45 motorway can now be used to hurry to
Frederikshavn, an important ferry port. The whitewashed
Krudttårnet (Gunpowder Tower) is part of the 17th-century
town fortress and was moved 270m in 1974 to allow the
dock area to expand. The Bangsbomuseet has a collection
on local history, some curios, and the reconstructed
remains of a Viking ship (open Jun–Oct daily 10:30–
17:00, Nov–May Tues–Sun 10:30–17:00). In front of the
town's beautiful church is a memorial to local men
drowned at sea.

Northward the road hugs Ålbæk Bay to reach
Skagen, neat and pretty, and Denmark's most northerly
town. It encompasses **Grenen** where the waters of the
North and Baltic seas meet. At nearby **Råbjerg Mile**, the
sand dunes are fantastic. Each year they move 15m
(49ft) east, as they have, inexorably, since the 16th century. Their formation and natural history is explored in
the Natural History Museum (open daily 10:00–18:00,
but until 16:00 in winter).

West of Råbjerg Mile is **Hirtshals**, a fishing and ferry

port where the aquarium is a major tourist attraction (open Jul–Aug daily 10:00–22:00, otherwise 10:00–17:00). West again, there are more superb dune systems at **Rubjerg Knude**, and a section of coast popular with holiday-makers, with numerous camp sites. Children will love **Sommerland** (open mid-May to Aug 10:00–18:00, but until 20:00 in Jul) at Fårup with its rides and play areas, while those interested in history will seek out **Børglum**, a bishop's residence from the 12th century which later became a monastery. The huge church and remains of the monastic buildings have been carefully restored.

Heading along the E39 back to Aalborg, a worthwhile stop-off is **Hjørring**, a quiet market town which is an open-air museum of modern Danish sculpture, over 100 pieces being dotted around the streets.

LIMFJORDEN ★

Limfjorden, which bisects northern Jutland, is now a centre for water sports. Some of its bays offer shelter for beginners, though the vast expanses of water close to the islands of **Mors** (*see* panel, page 66) and **Thyholm** offer a sterner challenge. The fjord reaches the North Sea at **Thyborøn**, a modern fishing port. The local area was heavily fortified during World War II as part of Germany's Atlantic Wall. A path threads its way through the bunkers and a museum looks at the history of the time. Look, too, for the curious Snail House decorated with shells from across the world.

On the fjord's southern shore **Lemvig** has a 'planet route' along which there are scale models of the planets of the solar system. **Struer** is the home of Bang and Olufsen, the electronics company which is the epitome of Danish style. From the town a road heads north across Limfjorden to Thyholm and the northern shore. **Skive**, at the base of the Salling Peninsula, is a neat town with a fine old church and a museum with Denmark's largest amber collection. From here a road crosses the peninsula and Limfjorden to reach the island of Mors where the **Jesperhus** is well worth a visit. It is Scandinavia's largest flower park with over 500,000 flowers across a 6ha

Opposite: *Evening light illuminates one of the stone ship graves at Lindholm Høje.*
Below: *This shop in Hirtshals is a clear in-dication of the continuing importance of fishing to the locals.*

GOD'S FIRST ATTEMPT

The Limfjorden island of Mors
(see page 65) is an almost
exact miniature of Jutland and
legend has it that before
embarking on the larger land
mass God first made Mors as a
practice attempt. It was so
beautiful he decided not to
throw it away, but placed it in
Limfjorden for safe keeping.

(15-acre) site. It also has an indoor zoo with free-flying
butterflies and parrots, monkeys and lizards, and a good
children's play area (open May–Oct daily 10:00–17:00,
but until 20:00 in Jul and Aug). From Skive a road hugs
the shore of Limfjorden, heading north past several interesting villages, including **Ålestrup** where Den Jydske
Rosenpark has 15,000 rose bushes and the Bicycle
Museum claims to be unique in Scandinavia.

At **Aggersund** the visitor can cross to the northern
shore – a left turn leads to **Aggersborg** where the largest
of Harald Bluetooth's four circular forts was built; sadly
nothing of the site remains as it was destroyed in 1086
– or head east to Aalborg.

A ferry crosses the narrow mouth of Limfjorden at
Thyborøn (see page 65), allowing visitors to reach
Vestervig which has the largest church of any Danish
village, a remnant of a monastery built in the 12th
century when this was an important port. Silting of
Limfjorden's narrow channel destroyed its prosperity.
The church is the legendary burial site of Liden Kirsten
and her lover Prince Buris who were buried end to end,
rather than side by side (see panel, page 69).

To the north, **Thisted** is a very ancient place, the
museum showing many Bronze-Age finds (open Apr–
Oct Tue–Sat 10:00–16:00). Now
its fine marina is a sailing centre.
North again, on the North Sea
coast, there are several villages
famous as windsurfing centres,
Klitmøller being the best known of
these. Nearby **Hanstholm** has
another museum to the German
Atlantic Wall (open Feb–May
daily 10:00–16:00, Jun–Aug daily
10:00–17:00, Sep–Oct daily
10:00–16:00), while at the other
(eastern) end of Vigsø Bay the massive cliffs of **Bulbjerg** offer fantastic
views of the North Sea and the
scenic Jutland coast.

Below: *The Dream Castle
of Bjørn Nørgaard at the
Nordjyllands Kunst-
museum (Museum of
Modern Art) in Aalborg.*

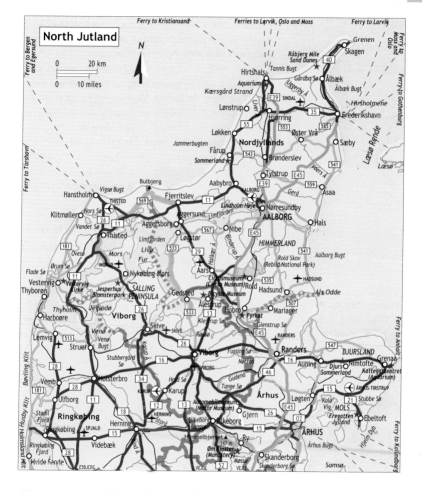

HIMMERLAND AND CENTRAL JUTLAND ★★

Immediately south of Aalborg lies the Himmerland region in which lies **Rold Skov**, Denmark's largest forest, covering an area of about 80km² (about 30 sq miles). The forest forms a part of **Rebild Bakker** (Rebild Hills), Denmark's only national park.

In the park are several museums and memorials to Danes who emigrated to the USA and who were responsible for buying the land that forms the park. One somewhat strange inclusion is a replica of the log cabin in which Abraham Lincoln was born. At the village of **Rold** there is Circus Museum (open May–Oct daily 11:00–16:00). Further south is

Above: *Children's farm park, north Jutland. The Danes have lots of attractions for children and strawmen like this are a common sight.*

Hobro, a pleasant but uninspiring town on the southwestern edge of which lies **Fyrkat**, one of the most interesting sites on Jutland. Although less well known than Trelleborg on Zealand (which has the advantage of being close to Copenhagen), Fyrkat is every bit as good (open Easter to mid-Oct daily 10:00–16:00, but until 17:00 Jun–Aug and 15:00 in Sep to mid-Oct). It is one of four circular forts known in Denmark, all of which are believed to have been constructed by Harald Bluetooth in about AD980. Although originally thought to have been used as barracks prior to an invasion of England, the forts are now believed to have been administrative centres – part of Harald's control structure for his kingdom. For lovers of eccentric sites, Hobro also has a museum dedicated to the use of gas in home and industry (open May–Sep daily 11:00–16:00).

To the east of Hobro, at **Mariager**, a trip on the paddle steamer *Svanen* is a gentle way to explore the Mariager Fjord (Jun–Aug, Tue, Thu and Sun). Heading south, visitors soon reach **Randers**, a market town which grew up at the point where the Gudenå (Denmark's longest river) meets the narrow extremity of Randers Fjord. Medieval Randers was a prosperous place and there are several buildings dating from this period. Sankt Martens Kirke dates from the 15th century, as do Helligåndshuset (Holy Ghost House, so called because it formed part of a monastery) and the magnificent Paaskesønnernes Gård, a three-storey, brick-built house. The town has area and history museums and a tropical zoo with snakes, iguanas, monkeys and rainforest plants (open Jun to mid-Aug daily 10:00–18:00, but closes at 16:00 the rest of the year). It also has something which must be unique in Europe: the local brewery is connected by underground pipes directly to the bars in Storegade.

West from Randers is **Viborg** which grew up in the 8th century at a junction of important cross-Jutland roads. The crypt of the twin-towered cathedral dates from the 12th century, but above ground it is a late 19th-century rebuilding. This rather severe edifice is enlivened inside by enthusiastic frescoes executed from 1899–1906 by Joakim Skovgaard. There is a museum to the artist close to the cathedral indicating that he had a much wider range of subject material than might be expected (open May–Sep daily 10:00–12:30 and 13:30–17:00, Oct–Apr 13:30–17:00 only).

Southwest of Viborg, at **Herning**, the Kunstmuseum, a little way east of the town, has a fine collection which began when a local shirt manufacturer used part of the profits to invest in a new generation of Danish artists. The main collection is in the old shirt factory, but impressive new buildings house further pieces. Close by, the pyramid and the circular, frieze-decorated building are dedicated to the work of Carl-Henning Pedersen and his wife (open May–Nov Tue–Sun, and Mon in Jul, 10:00–16:30; Dec–Apr 12:00–16:30). Herning also has a fine sculpture park, the Geometric Garden, and Elia, an extraordinary work that involves fire and lightning. As the town is also home to Denmark's National Photographic Museum (open Tue–Sun, and Mon in Jun, 11:00–16:30) and a fine

Left: *These ultra-modern buildings house the work of Carl-Henning Pedersen and his wife at Herning.*

Above: *The theatre in Århus stands close to the city's cathedral.*

History Museum which includes outdoor exhibits (open Tue–Fri, and Mon in Jul, 10:00–17:00; Sat and Sun 11:00–17:00), a day could easily be spent in this exceptional town.

West of Herning, **Ringkøbing** grew up as a trading port. Its position, in a fjord virtually enclosed by crab-like pincers of sand, offered it the advantage of shelter from the notoriously stormy North Sea. But when in the 17th century shifting sands caused the outlet to the North Sea to close, the town's future was jeopardized. Not until 1931, when the lock at **Hvide Sande** was made, was Ringkøbing's future made secure. Hvide Sande itself is a fishing port with a small museum to the fishing industry. The (very) early morning fish market is a lively place, assailing all the senses (well, smell, sight and hearing if not necessarily taste and touch). **Holmsland Klit**, further to the south, is popular with windsurfers.

ÅRHUS ★★★

Denmark's second city was founded in the 10th century and become prosperous as the leading port on Jutland's east coast, its sheltered harbour and lack of a fjord aiding trade. When sea travel was the major link between Jutland and the outlying islands and capital, Århus boomed, growing into Denmark's second city. It is also the seat of the country's second university. The city's commercial development means that there is no ancient heart as there is at Aalborg. Århus is a bustling, modern town which requires more determination to unlock its secrets. The best place to start is **Domkirkeplads (Store Torv)**, around which the city grew. The huge red-brick cathedral – it has the largest nave of any cathedral in Denmark – dominates the square. Though severe outside, the interior is light and elegant. The Gothic altar is the greatest treasure (perhaps in the country), a late 15th-century masterpiece of Bernt Notke, a Lübeck master. The other great treasures are the 15th-century frescoes. Though some of the paintings have a moral message, others indicate that the artist had a terrific sense of humour. Also in the square is the theatre, the excavated remains of Viking Århus (the **Vikinge-museet**, situated beneath the Unibank at No. 6, open Mon–Fri, except Thu, from 10:00–16:00 and Thu 10:00–17:30), and Denmark's only **Kvindemuseet** (Women's Museum), dedicated to women's history and art (open Jun–Aug daily 10:00–17:00; Sep–May Tue–Sun 10:00–16:00). The museum has an excellent café. To the west of Domskirkeplads, **Vor Frue Kirke** dates from the 12th century and has another fine altar. The **Natural History Museum** in Århus is a superb museum on Danish wildlife, including the evolution of the Danish landscapes. Open daily 10:00–16:00 (17:00 in Jul and Aug).

Further from the centre the **Moesgård Museum** explores the area's prehistoric and Viking past. The main attraction here is Grauballe Man, excavated from a peat bog in 1952 and second only to Tollund Man in preservation (open Apr–Sep daily 10:00–17:00; Oct–Mar

> **HOLMSLAND KLIT**
>
> Holmsland Klit is the slender finger of land, 35km (22 miles) long, which separates Ringkøbing Fjord from the North Sea. Though it is very narrow, the white sand is piled in dunes which prevent drivers from getting more than a glimpse of the sea, though the fjord views are terrific. Holmsland Klit is popular with both beach lovers and windsurfers.

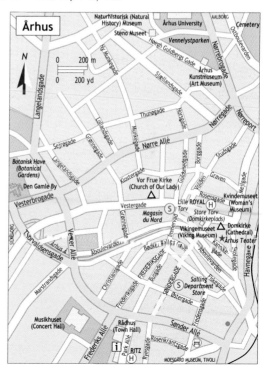

ÅRHUS TOWN HALL

One of the city's most controversial buildings is the Rådhus
(Town Hall), designed by Arne
Jacobsen and built in 1941. Its
gaunt, almost Soviet, function-
alism contrasts starkly with the
clock tower where the external
ribbing looks unfinished.
Inside the building is light and
expansive and has a thought-
provoking mural.

DEN GAMLE BY

As well as the houses and their
furnishings the Den Gamle By
buildings also house other collections – the National Museum
of clocks and watches, a toy
museum and collections of
silver and porcelain. During the
summer and at Christmas the
authenticity of the site is
enhanced by characters in period costume. Visitors can then
tour the site by pony and trap.

Tue–Sun 10:00–16:00). Århus also has its own **Tivoli**
amusement park (open Apr–Aug daily 12:00–21:00 or
even later; weekends only in Apr) and a museum to the
history of firefighting. Best of all is **Den Gamle By**, one of
Denmark's outstanding museums and certainly the best
outside Copenhagen. The 'old town' is a collection of 75
historically important houses from across Denmark,
uprooted, re-erected and furnished in period style to
create a complete town (open Jan daily 11:00–15:00;
Feb–Mar daily 10:00–16:00; Apr–Jun and Sep–Nov daily
10:00–17:00; Jul–Aug daily 09:00–18:00; Dec daily
10:00–19:00). Den Gamle By stands in the Botanical
Gardens, a very beautiful park. Equally as good is the
city's University Park, to the north of the cathedral. As
well as excellent parkland there are natural history, art
and science museums here.

Northeast of Århus lie **Djursland** and **Mols**, a rounded
peninsula of Jutland worth visiting for the white sand
beaches and peaceful country. At **Ebeltoft** the *Fregatten
Jylland* is a restored 19th-century wooden frigate. The
town also has an interesting Glasmuseet which explores
various uses of glass. At **Grenaa** there are old houses,
one of which is now a museum of local history and the
fishing industry, and a good aquarium of Kattegat
marine life. Children may enjoy the aquarium, but will
definitely enjoy **Djurs
Sommerland** near Nim-
tofte, which has rides and
play areas for all ages.

From Århus ferries cross
to **Samsø**, an island
halfway between Jutland
and Zealand. Samsø is
renowned for its early
potato crop (the earliest in
northern Europe, it is
claimed), and Nordby, a
very pretty village, for its
prehistoric sites and for
some lovely scenery.

Left: *Tollund Man, one of the most remarkable and moving archaeological discoveries in Europe.* **Opposite:** *A cobbled street in Den Gamle By, the Old Town, which brings alive Denmark's past with its collection of old houses and period furnishings.*

SILKEBORG AND THE LAKES ★★★

West of Århus lies **Silkeborg**, a new town dating only from the 1840s when a paper mill was built beside the Remstrup River. The mill owner (and, therefore, founder of the town) was Michael Drewsen whose statue can be seen in the Torvet (central square). Silkeborg has none of the charm of the medieval centres that grace many Jutland towns, but is nonetheless very pretty due, in part, to its beautiful setting where the river meets Silkeborg Langsø (lake). Arriving from Århus, visitors cross a bridge over the Remstrup and turn left to reach the Tourist Information Office and the **museum**, the town's major attraction (open May–Oct daily 10:00–17:00; Oct–Apr Wed, Sat and Sun 12:00–16:00). The museum explores the area's history from prehistoric times to the 19th century, but the main interest is **Tollund Man**, the best preserved of all European bog people. Discovered in 1950 by local peat-cutters, the body was so perfect that it is surprising a murder inquiry was not begun. The body is believed to date from about 400BC and is of a ritual sacrifice victim; the rope used to hang him is still in place. Ritual sacrifice rather than murder or execution is suspected as the victim was treated with kindness after his death. His eyes and mouth were closed and he was placed in a sleeping position, not thrown into the bog. So perfect is the preservation, the stubble on the man's chin is visible – viewing Tollund Man is a very moving experience.

TOLLUND MAN'S LAST MEAL

An analysis of the contents of the Tollund Man's stomach showed that his last meal consisted of porridge made from barley and a variety of other seeds. He had eaten no meat.

Above: *Modern windmills. Denmark went straight from old windmills for grinding to new windmills for power production without an intermediate phase of no windmills.*

South of Tollund Man's last resting place the **Silkeborg Kunstmuseum** has work by Asgar Jorn, locally born and one of the best-known COBRA artists, as well as others of the movement (open Apr–Oct Tue–Sun 10:00–17:00; Nov–Mar Tue–Fri 12:00–16:00, Sat and Sun 10:00–17:00). A little further south is AQUA, a new site where visitors can view otters, beavers, ducks and fish from a submerged building, an unlikely idea brought to fulfilment by Danish ingenuity and style (open Jul–Aug daily 10:00–18:00; Sep to mid-Dec Mon–Fri 10:00–16:00 and Jan–Jun Sat and Sun 10:00–17:00).

Silkeborg is a good centre from which to explore the lovely lake and mountain scenery to the southeast. The very best exploration uses the *Hjejlen* to reach Himmelbjerg (*see* panel, this page). On Himmelbjerg or in the surrounding country, there is plenty of scope for walking. Since the lakes are perfect for canoeing, this makes the area excellent for more active visitors. The views, from both hilltop and lake surface, are stunning.

At **Ry**, another good exploring centre, there is a museum which looks at the history and natural history of the lakes. West of the town there is a fine old windmill, now part of a museum complex that includes one dedicated to clog-making (open May–Sep Tues–Sun 10:00–17:00). It is claimed that in the 19th century half the population of Ry were involved in this industry. South of the town are the ruins of the **Øm Monastery** which dates from the 12th century.

One final site is worth mentioning: the Jysk Motor Museum at **Gjern**, northeast of Silkeborg, where enthusiasts can enjoy around 140 vehicles dating back to the 1900s (open Apr to mid-May Sat and Sun 10:00–17:00; mid-May to mid-Sep daily 10:00–17:00; mid-Sep to Oct Sat and Sun 10:00 to 17:00).

North Jutland at a Glance

Jutland is the cooler, wetter side of Denmark, so best in summer. The area, particularly the beaches of the west coast, is popular with Germans for whom Jutland is a short drive. Spring and autumn are pleasant, but winter can be cold and windy, a time for visiting museums rather than walking.

There are airports at Aalborg and Århus for domestic flights from Copenhagen. The airport at Billund can also be used to reach north Jutland. The E45 gives a connection from Little Belt bridge. Road travel to the west is rather slower, though the roads are good. A railway line follows the E45, and there is also a line to the west coast.

Reasonable bus service between the bigger towns, but the service to outlying villages is limited. The road system is good and much preferred.

As can be expected, the best hotels are in the big towns. Some west coast holiday towns have good hotels too.

LUXURY

Hotel Royal, Store Torv 4, 8100 Århus, tel: 86 120011, fax: 86 760404. One of the best in Jutland. Central location in the cathedral square. The city casino is in the hotel.

MID-RANGE

Radisson SAS Limfjord Hotel, Ved Stranden 14, 9000 Aalborg, tel: 98 164333, fax: 98 161747. Central, pleasant rooms. The car park (shared with the casino) tends to be full, forcing visitors to use the expensive one across the road.

Palads Hotel, Sankt Mathias Gade 5, 8800 Viborg, tel: 86 623700, fax: 86 624046. A Best Western near the station. Well-appointed rooms.

BUDGET

Hotel Eyde, Torvet 1, 7400 Herning, tel: 97 221800, fax: 97 210165. Delightful old hotel in the main square. Good rooms, cheerful staff.

Aalborg Sømanshjem, Østerbro 27, 9000 Aalborg, tel: 98 121900, fax: 98 117697. Just east of the centre. Cheap, cheerful and very pleasant.

Aalborg and Århus in particular have a range of prices and styles. Especially good is:

Kniv & Gaffel, Maren Turis Gade 10, 9000 Aalborg, tel: 98 166972. A delightful place (the name means Knife and Fork). Serves Danish cooking.

In Århus 'City-Vest' is a large complex near the centre. In the centre are two departmental stores, Magasin du Nord and Salling. Most other towns and villages have local craft outlets.

Aalborg and Århus offer city tours (by bus or horse-drawn carriage in Århus) and excursions to local places of interest.

Tourist Information Office: Østerågade 8, 9000 Aalborg, tel: 99 306090, fax: 98 166922.

Town Halls:
8000 Århus, tel: 89 406700, fax: 86 129590;
Torvet 1a, 7400 Herning, tel: 96 272222, fax: 96 272223;
Tørvebryggen 12, 8900 Randers, tel: 86 424477, fax: 86 406004;
Åhavevej 2a, 8600 Silkeborg, tel: 86 821911, fax: 86 810983;
Rådhuspladsen, 7600 Struer, tel: 97 850795, fax: 97 851713;
Stor Torv 6, 7700 Thisted, tel: 97 921900, fax: 97 925604;
Nytorv 9, 8800 Viborg, tel: 87 253075, fax: 86 600238.

ÅRHUS	J	F	M	A	M	J	J	A	S	O	N	D
AVERAGE TEMP. °C	0	-1	2	6	11	15	17	16	13	8	5	2
AVERAGE TEMP. °F	32	30	36	43	52	59	63	61	55	46	41	36
RAINFALL mm	55	38	31	37	29	47	75	70	66	62	58	50
RAINFALL in	2.2	1.5	1.2	1.5	1.1	1.9	3.0	2.8	2.6	2.4	2.3	2.0

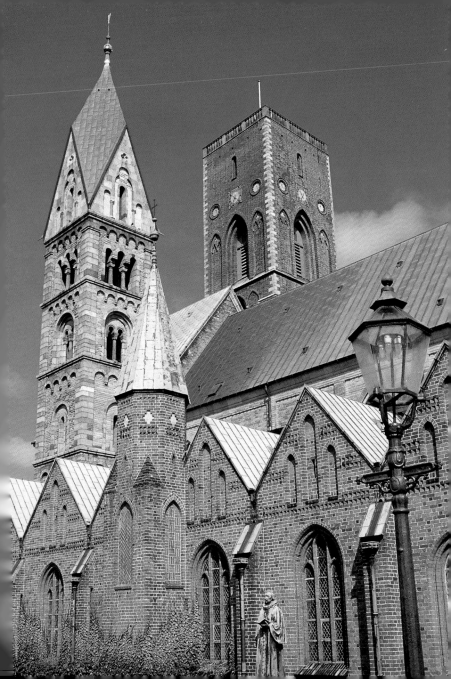

4
South Jutland

To the south of the E20 motorway the landscape of Jutland changes subtly. Although the interior is still pastoral, the farmland broken up with patches of woodland (though there are fewer patches than in the north), the coastal scenery is different. On the west coast the beaches and dunes are replaced by salt marshes and water meadows, while the east coast is deeply indented by fjords. The E20 gives easy access to **Kolding**, **Esbjerg** and **Vejle**, the latter a centre for visiting **Jelling** and Billund (where **Legoland** is Denmark's most famous visitor attraction). To the west **Ribe** is a highlight, though the 'island' of **Rømø** is equally entrancing. Southern Jutland has fewer 'must-see' sites; the fluid nature of Denmark's border with Germany means that towns here bore the brunt of conflict, and this is reflected in their lack of historical interest. As always there are exceptions to this generalization: **Aabenraa** and **Sønderborg** repay the time spent in visiting.

JELLING AND BILLUND ★★★

Not only is **Jelling** one of the highlights of Jutland, but one of the most interesting in the entire country. The interest centres on the rune stones which stand close to the church, itself set between two huge mounds; the whole complex is now a UNESCO World Heritage Site. Jelling was the royal capital of King Gorm who died in the 950s. He is believed to have been buried within an existing Bronze-Age tumulus at the head of a stone ship. Gorm raised the first rune stone himself.

North Sea — Aalborg — SWEDEN — Århus — **DENMARK** — Copenhagen — Esbjerg — Odense — Bornholm — **GERMANY**

DON'T MISS

★★★ **Jelling:** finest rune stones in Denmark; one of Europe's great historical sites.
★★★ **Ribe:** marvellous old Viking town
★★★ **Legoland:** it's hardly credible what can be achieved with plastic bricks.
★★ **Rømø:** very attractive and quiet island.
★ **Vejle:** charming little town with delightful old courtyard at its heart.

Opposite: *St Mary's Tower and, beyond, the square-cut Commoners' Tower dominate the beautiful Romanesque cathedral at Ribe.*

THE RUNE STONES
TRANSLATED

The smaller stone is engraved 'King Gorm raised this for Thyra, his wife, Denmark's glory'. The longer one says 'King Harald raised this to the memory of Gorm, his father, and Thyra, his mother. Harald won all Denmark and Norway and made the Danes Christian'.

VITUS BERING

Horsens was the birthplace of Vitus Bering who has given his name to the narrow straits between Russia and Alaska. Bering was employed in the Czarist navy and commanded two expeditions in the northern Pacific, the second 'discovering' Alaska which Russia occupied, but later sold to the USA. Returning from the second expedition, Bering and many of his men died of scurvy in the Commander Islands. Recently his body was exhumed and his face reconstructed from the skull. To everyone's surprise it was not the same as the drawing long held to be Bering's likeness.

Harald Bluetooth, Gorm's son, enlarged the burial mound, but when he converted to Christianity he moved his father's and mother's remains to a wooden church he built between the mounds. Harald erected the second rune stone. The church, built on the site of Harald's first wooden structure, has some of the oldest frescoes in Denmark, dating from the 12th century.

Close to Jelling, at **Givskud**, there is a large safari park with over 1000 animals (open May–Sep daily 10:00–18:00, later in Aug). In the opposite direction is **Vejle**. Here Den Smidtske Gård is a restored late 18th-century merchant's house, now part of the town museum (open May–Oct Tue–Sat 13:00–17:00). The town also has a Golf Museum (*see* Munkebjerg Hotel, page 85). In Sankt Nicolai Kirke, an Iron-Age bog woman is on display and the skulls of 23 persons, believed to have been executed felons, are set in the north wall. Northeast of Vejle is **Horsens**, where Søndergade is said to be Denmark's widest street. It is crowded with fine 18th- and 19th-century houses. The half-timbered Monbergs Gåde is among the most beautiful, but Claus Cortsens Gård, three-storeyed and onion-dome-topped, in Sundvej is the most fascinating building in the town. The Art Museum has an excellent modern section (open May–Sep Tue–Sun 11:00–17:00, Oct–Apr Sat and Sun 11:00–16:00).

South of Vejle, **Fredericia** began life in the 17th century as a fortress town, the fortress seeing service against both Swedes and Germans. This lively history is explored in the town museum. Also to the south is **Kolding**, once a border town between Denmark and Schleswig. Koldinghus, the town castle, stands beside a lake. During the Napoleonic Wars, Spanish soldiers were garrisoned here: they lit a fire to ward off winter's chills, but the fire went out of control and virtually razed the building. Only in 1890 was restoration begun, and it is still in progress. The town also has fine old houses, particularly Borchs Gård, built in 1595 and claimed to have the most elaborately decorated façade in the country. There is also a huge and excellent art and craft gallery (Kunstmuseet Trapholt, open daily

10:00–17:00) and the Geografisk Have, a geographical garden with plants from across the world.

Heading west from Vejle the visitor reaches **Billund**, separated from Jelling by a few kilometres, but as far away as possible in cultural terms. **Legoland** is the home of a modern phenomenon. In the 1930s Ole Kirk Christiansen, a local carpenter, made some wooden toys to stave off the poverty of the depression years. As interest grew he expanded his range, giving his company the name Lego from *leg godt*, play well. By the 1940s Lego had begun to produce the first plastic, injection-moulded, interlocking bricks. It still made wooden toys, but ceased production in the 1960s when a fire destroyed that part of the factory. Today Lego is Denmark's best-known

CLIMATE

As with the north of Jutland the nearness of the North Sea dominates the weather. Be prepared for **westerly winds** and some **rainfall**. In summer days can be warm and sunny making the west coast delightful.

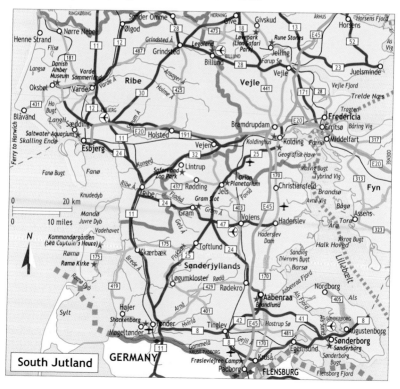

South Jutland

Above: *Denmark is famous as the birthplace of Lego. Legoland, built with millions of the plastic bricks, is the best-known tourist site on Jutland.*

company, selling on every continent except Antarctica. The park shows what can be done with more than 30 million bricks, with replicas of the world's famous landmarks. Titania's Palace is a miniature palace and there is an excellent doll museum. But Legoland is more than a 'look at' site. There are rides and play areas, one of which includes the construction of programmable robots (open Mar–Oct daily 10:00–20:00, but until 21:00 in Jul and Aug, and until 18:00 in Oct).

FANØ'S CUNNING PURCHASE

Offshore from Esbjerg lies the holiday island of Fanø. In 1741 its royal owner, King Christian VI, decided to sell the island by auction, a move which worried the islanders who feared purchase by a wealthy merchant and the end of their quiet, tax-free life. It is said that on the night before the auction young Fanø women kept would-be buyers up late drinking and canoodling, then changed their watches as they slept. The prospective buyers turned up at the auction only to discover that the islanders had already bought the island.

ESBJERG ★

Visitors from Britain reaching Denmark by ferry from Harwich arrive in **Esbjerg**, the country's fifth city and home to a large North Sea fishing fleet. Not surprisingly the town has a fisheries museum and a good saltwater aquarium with both fish and seals (open daily 10:00–17:00 or 18:00; seals fed at 11:00 and 14:30). The town museum has the best amber collection in Denmark (though that suggestion is unlikely to find favour with the management of the Danish Amber Museum at **Oksbøl**, to the northwest of Esbjerg). Esbjerg is a thoroughly modern place, though the spacious, elegant central square is more old-fashioned, with its statue of King Christian IX, who granted Esbjerg its first charter. Look, too, for the **Vandtårn**, the water tower, built in 1897 but crenellated in medieval fashion, a wonderfully extravagant idea for so utilitarian a building. From the top there is a fine view of the town. There is a good art museum, but by far the most striking work can be seen beside the sea on the coast road heading northwest. Here stands *Mennesket ved Havet,* Man meets the Sea. The work, created by Svend Wiig Hansen in 1995, comprises four white seated figures, each 9m (30ft) high.

North of Esbjerg at **Varde** there are some fine old houses. Children will love nearby **Sommerland** with its rides and play areas – parents will love the idea that everything is free once the entrance fee is paid (open May–Sep daily 10:00–18:00). Other family-based sites around Esbjerg include the Safari and Zoo Park at **Lintrup**, to the east. Lintrup is also home to the Welling's Landbysmuseum, the collection of the painter Søren Welling who assembled artefacts of all kinds relating to the old way of life of Danish country folk (open Jan–Dec daily 10:00–17:00). Not far from Lintrup, at **Jels**, the Orion Planetarium has regular shows of the stars and astronomical phenomena (open May–Sep Tue–Wed and Sat–Sun, also Wed 19:00–22:00; open daily in July 11:00–16:30 and Oct–Apr Wed 19:00–22:00, Fri 11:00–16:00).

RIBE ★★★

Tucked so neatly away from the south Jutland road system that it is possible for visitors to pass without realizing they have done so, **Ribe** is Denmark's (and Scandinavia's) oldest city and one of its most picturesque. Founded in the early 8th century around a river bridge and expanded in the Viking era as a trading centre, Ribe now has a wealth of old buildings protected by law. The **cathedral** dates in part from the 12th century, but the apse decoration of murals and stained glass by Carl-Henning Pedersen date from the 1980s. Look, too, for the famous 'Cat Head Door' with its superb tympanum and pediment. The view of the town and local country makes the long climb to the tower worthwhile.

Ribe has two sites that celebrate its Viking past. The **Vikinger** has a reconstruction of a country market with laden

THE TØNDER FESTIVAL

On the last weekend of August each year Tønder (*see* page 83) becomes the centre for a folk musical festival which has grown into one of the most important in Europe. All forms of folk are included, as well as jazz and gospel, the festival attracting both 'unknown' and world-famous performers.

Below: *King Christian IX trots (in statue form at least) through Esbjerg's Torvet.*

ship (open Apr–Oct daily 10:00–16:00, but till 18:00 in Jul and Aug); the **Vikingecentre** has a longhouse and characters in period costume demonstrating Viking skills (open May, Jun, Sep Mon–Fri 10:00–15:30 and daily in Jul and Aug 11:00–17:00). The town also has a good art museum and a museum of dolls and toys (open Jan–Mar Sun–Fri 13:00–16:00; Apr–May daily 13:00–17:00; Jun–Aug daily 10:00–12:00, 13:00–17:00; Sep–Oct daily 13:00–17:00; Nov–Dec Sun–Fri 13:00–16:00). Det Gamle Rådhus (the old town hall), a fine 15th-century building and the oldest town hall in Denmark, also has a small museum with a history collection that includes a spiked mace and a rather macabre executioner's sword.

Yet for all that the museums are worthwhile, what is best is to wander the exquisite streets of Ribe enjoying the views. Virtually the whole town is pedestrianized and is a total joy, but to see the best, follow the night watchman as he sings his way around his beat. He can be followed at 20:00 and 22:00 from June to August, and at 22:00 in late May and early September.

Below: *The cathedral towers peep over the old houses in this view of the centre of Ribe, one of Denmark's most interesting cities.*

THE FAR SOUTH ★★

South of Ribe a narrow causeway pokes out into the North Sea, leading to the 'island' of **Rømø**. Extending from the causeway are wooden groynes set to trap silt and so reclaim land. The resulting semi-marsh is popular with sea birds and waders. Arriving on Rømø is like

reaching a different world, the island being entirely rural with thatched cottages and even village ponds. The western side, facing the North Sea, is lined with beaches and is extremely popular with German tourists. Heading north from the causeway's end visitors will find **Kommandørgården**, the sea captain's house, dating from the mid-18th century (when it was built by Hareke Thades, a whaling captain) and now part of the National Museum (open May–Oct daily 10:00–18:00, but until 15:00 in Oct). South from the causeway's end is Rømø Kirke with a small World War II cemetery. Much older graves have yielded the grave slabs which line the churchyard's north wall. These are of Danish whalers active between 1650 and 1850.

Above: *The simple, dignified church of Rømø. The churchyard holds the graves of whalers and Allied servicemen.*

Back on the mainland the visitor can call in at Hjemsted Oldtidspark near **Skærbæk** where the Iron Age is recreated. Visitors can try their hand at archery and paddling a dugout canoe (open mid-May to Sep daily 11:00–18:00). To the south lies **Tønder**, close to the German border. In early medieval times Tønder was a port – an important one, but one which was often flooded. To reduce flooding a series of dykes were dug, but these pushed the sea back so that the town traded dry feet for loss of trade. In the 17th century it was the most important lace-making centre in Europe; the wealth created was reflected in the array of fine houses. Lace-making takes pride of place in the town's museum (open Mon–Fri 10:00–17:00). The town also has a Zeppelin Museum in what was a German World War I airship base. Det Gamle Apotek, the old pharmacy, is also worth visiting. Built in 1691 as a pharmacy, the building now houses various collections including toys, dolls and Christmas lights (open May–Oct Sat and Sun 12:00–17:00).

Near Tønder, **Møgeltønder** has a cobbled, tree-lined main street with its thatched cottages and the extraordinary village church. Inside there are beautiful frescoes and paintings. There is also the private seating of the Schack family who built Schackenborg, a castle that is now home to Queen Margrethe's youngest son, Prince Joachim, and his wife. Further west, **Højer** has the only thatched town hall in Denmark and is a centre for birdwatching on the salt marshes, which are famous for waders and the 'black sun' of roosting starlings.

THE 1777 DISASTER

Many of the gravestones on the Rømø churchyard wall are dated 1777. In June of that year 28 ships were trapped in ice between Spitsbergen and east Greenland. Fifteen ships were eventually freed, but the rest were crushed and lost, over 300 men dying of cold and hunger. Fifty of these men were from Rømø, some of them commemorated on the slabs. One Rømø survivor was Anders Mickelsen List who was only 12. He eventually became a whale captain and is buried in the churchyard.

Above: *A whaler gravestone in Rømø churchyard. The stones give an insight into the harsh lives of Denmark's Arctic whalers.*

TILTING AT RINGS

Throughout Europe in early medieval times tournaments were held at which knights would joust or tilt for a ring suspended between two poles. In southern Jutland this sport continues, a summer-long series of tilts being held, events attracting up to 400 riders. Each rider uses a pointed spear to try to collect the ring, and marks are awarded for style as well as success.

North of Tønder is **Løgumkloster** where in August each year a huge horse and flea market is held. So famous is it that a Jutland saying notes 'If I don't see you before, I'll see you at Kloster market'. The beautiful village church is almost all that now remains of a 12th-century Cistercian monastery.

On the other side of the peninsula the island of **Als** is separated from the mainland by the narrow Als Sund which is guarded by the factory-like castle of **Sønderborg**, a pleasant seaside town. In 1864 the Danes lost the battle of Dybbøl to the Germans. Sønderborg was almost flattened by artillery and then occupied until 1918. This history is explored in the castle museum (open May–Sep 10:00–17:00, Oct–Mar 13:00–16:00, Apr 10:00–16:00), while the Dybbøl battlefield has a centre which retells the story of the battle. Another memory of conflict is the preserved Frøeslevlejren camp, near **Padborg**, built by the Nazis in 1944 for Danish political prisoners (open daily 10:00–17:00). Very different is Danfoss Universe, a science and technology based theme park near Nordborg in southern Jutland (north of Sønderborg). Open daily 10:00–18:00 (mid-Jun to mid-Aug 10:00–20:00). The Universe stands in a large park.

Aabenraa, set in a deep indent on Jutland's east coast, was once a major trading port, but was occupied after the 1864 Dybbøl defeat. A German daily newspaper is still printed here. At the heart of the city is the early 19th-century Brandlund Castle. Look too for the delightful night watchman's memorial. North of Aabenraa, **Haderslev** has an impressive cathedral and a fine pottery museum (Ehlers-Samlingen) housed in a 16th-century half-timbered house. Finally, to complete this tour of Jutland's south country, head west to **Gram** where the manor house, standing in beautiful grounds, is now a fascinating museum of Jutland's geology and natural history.

South Jutland at a Glance

As for North Jutland, summer is the most popular time, with spring and autumn pleasant, and winter cold and windy.

GETTING THERE

There are airports at Billund and Sønderborg, the former giving access to Legoland and the north, the latter set at the southern end of Jutland. The airports at Århus and Odense and the E45 or E20 can also be used. The E45 runs down the east of Jutland, and the E45 crosses from the Little Belt to Esbjerg. A railway line follows the E45 on the eastern side.

GETTING AROUND

Reasonable bus service between the bigger towns, but the service to outlying villages is limited. The road system is good and much preferred.

WHERE TO STAY

There are good hotels in Esbjerg and towns of eastern Jutland, and in some villages.

LUXURY
Radisson SAS Koldingfjord Hotel, Fjordvej 154, 6000 Kolding, tel: 75 510000, fax: 75 510022. Set in protected forest beside the fjord. Probably the best in south Jutland.
Hotel Dagmar, Torvet, 6760 Ribe, tel: 75 420033, fax: 75 423652. The oldest hotel in Denmark, in the oldest town. Absolutely charming, it offers an unforgettable stay.

Hotel Legoland, Aastvej 10, 7190 Billund, tel: 75 331244, fax: 75 353810. For those who want to stay on site. Upper mid-range to expensive family rooms in the Kids House which overlooks the park.

MID-RANGE
Hotel Ansgar, Skolegade 36, Esbjerg, tel: 75128244, fax: 75139540. Good place for those arriving on the ferry, or those looking for a base on the west coast. Slightly faded, but very pleasant. Good restaurant.
Munkebjerg Hotel, Munkebjergvej 125, 7100 Vejle, tel: 76 428500, fax: 75 720886. Ideal for golf enthusiasts as this hotel houses Europe's only museum of golf.

BUDGET
Hotel Lakolk, Lakolk 150, 6792 Rømø, tel: 74 755145, fax: 74 755987. Very neat and pleasant hotel on the west coast of the island. Good facilities.

WHERE TO EAT

All the main towns and villages have excellent restaurants. In the old town centres – Ribe, Tønder – it is possible to eat in delightful surroundings.

SHOPPING

Aabenraa and Sønderborg are large enough to have shopping centres. The smaller towns and villages have craft outlets.

TOURS AND EXCURSIONS

Tourist Information Offices have details of tours and excursions. There are tours to Ribe and Legoland from most of the nearby large towns.

USEFUL CONTACTS

Tourist Information Offices:
HP Hanssens Gade 5, 6200 Aabenraa, tel: 74 623500, fax: 74 630744;
c/o Legoland, 7190 Billund, tel: 75 331333, fax: 75 353179;
Skolegade 33, 6700 Esbjerg, tel: 75 125599, fax: 75 122767;
Honnøkajen 1, 6100 Haderslev, tel: 74 525550, fax: 74 534667;
Møllegade 12, 6280 Højer, tel: 74 782993, fax: 74 782893;
Torvet 3, 6760 Ribe, tel: 75 421500, fax: 75 424078;
Rådhustorvet 7, 6400 Sønderborg, tel: 74 423555, fax: 74 425747;
Torvet 1, 6270 Tønder, tel: 74 721220, fax: 74 720900;
Havnebyvej 30, Tvismark, 6792 Rømø, tel: 74 755130, fax: 74 755031.

ESBJERG	J	F	M	A	M	J	J	A	S	O	N	D
AVERAGE TEMP. °C	0	0	4	8	12	15	17	17	15	10	5	2
AVERAGE TEMP. °F	32	32	39	46	54	59	63	63	59	50	41	36
RAINFALL mm	55	45	40	40	43	43	75	80	85	78	70	66
RAINFALL in	2.2	1.8	1.6	1.6	1.7	1.7	3.0	3.2	3.4	3.1	2.8	2.6

HANS CHRISTIAN
ANDERSEN

5
Fyn

First we must decide what to call Denmark's second largest island. In Danish it is Fyn, often 'translated' into English as Funen, though quite why when the Danish name is so conveniently pronounced is unclear. So, Fyn it is. Fyn is divided from Jutland by the **Lillebælt**, the Little Belt, and from Zealand by the **Storebælt**, the Great Belt, each of which links the Kattegat to the true Baltic Sea. The Little Belt, only 700m (765yd) wide at its narrowest point, was first bridged in 1935. Thirty-five years later it was crossed again by the bridge that allows the E20 motorway to reach Fyn on its way to the new Great Belt crossing. The island the E20 crosses has the most fertile soil in Denmark. That, and its position at the heart of the country, explains the number of castles and mansions.

The island's fertility has drawn man to Fyn since the earliest times. Though there is not the concentration of Viking sites that Jutland boasts, the **Ladby** and **Glavendrup** sites are unique, and Fyn's prehistoric sites are the finest in Denmark. **Nyborg** has a castle important to Denmark's history, but it is another castle, that at **Egeskov**, which is the most impressive. It is a fairy-tale castle, appropriately so as that master of fairy tales, Hans Christian Andersen, was born on Fyn. **Odense**, his birthplace, is the island's biggest and most splendid town, but the artistic centre of **Faaborg** cannot be ignored.

What must also not be ignored is the cluster of islands off Fyn's south coast – **Tåsinge** and **Ærø**, and most particularly **Langeland**.

DON'T MISS

*** Odense: a beautiful city, the birthplace of Hans Christian Andersen.
*** Egeskov: one of the best – if not the best – castles in Denmark, with something for all the family.
** Faaborg: lovely little town which is an open-air museum of Danish sculpture.
** Langeland: some of the best beaches in Denmark on a really pretty island.
* Ladbyskibet: fascinating Viking site, the only ship burial found so far in Denmark.

Opposite: *The statue of Hans Christian Andersen in Odense.*

Above: *Enjoying a coffee in the square in front of Odense's Rådhus.*

ODENSE ★★★

Odense, by a very considerable margin the largest town on Fyn, is also at the island's centre, making it an excellent base for touring as well as a destination in its own right. In Viking times the town was a centre for the worship of Odin, the god of war, and later the site of one of the four circular forts constructed by Harald Bluetooth.

In 1086 Odense's fortunes improved, ironically as a result of a murder. Knud II had become king in 1080. His reign was an odd mix of the tyrannical and the ecclesiastical. Knud was keen to improve the authority of the Christian church, but also introduced heavy taxes (brutally collected) to finance raids on England. On one raid he brought back the relics of St Alban for which he built a church in Odense. In 1102, not long after he had been murdered, Knud was canonized and his shrine brought pilgrims, prosperity following in their wake, to Odense. The city's position, at the heart of Denmark, maintained its prosperity in medieval times, but the lack of a harbour led to a decline until 1804, when a canal was opened to Odense Fjord to the north. Today Odense is a well-heeled university town, a spacious elegant city with a wealth of corporate artwork that adds to the air of sophistication. Many visitors arrive to find Hans Christian Andersen, the city's most famous son, and rightly so. But there is far more to Odense than that.

The Gothic, brick-built **Sankt Knuds Kirke** (Cathedral of St Knud) dominates the city centre. Built on the site of a church raised by the sainted king, it dates from the 12th century and is one of Denmark's most important churches. Inside there is a magnificent **gilded altar**, and a triptych that is the masterwork of woodcarver Klaus Berg who created it in 1521 for Queen Christine. A complete contrast, but equally compelling, are the **skeletal remains** of St Knud in a Romanesque reliquary in the cathedral's crypt. The second reliquary holds remains which are thought to be those of Knud's brother, Benedict, but which some experts believe to be those of St Alban.

Across from the cathedral is **Flakhaven**, the main square where modern sculptures stand infront of the 19th-century **Rådhus**. The Rådhus houses the city's Tourist Information Office (entrance around the corner in Vestergade). Heading east between the Rådhus and the cathedral, the visitor passes a **statue** of the martyred St Knud before reaching **Sankt Albani Kirke**, an early 20th-century Roman Catholic church which takes its name from the site of the murder. Turn left along Torvegade, taking care when crossing it, to reach Hans Jensens Stræde, passing **Fyrtøjet** (the Tinderbox), a children's culture house, where families participate in theatre and visual arts based on Andersen's fairy tales. Almost next door, in the achingly quaint Hans Jensens Stræde – the pastel-coloured houses looking like part of a fairy tale – is

> ### CARL NIELSEN
>
> Carl Nielsen (1865–1931) was actually born a few kilometres south of Odense, but played in the city's Regimented Band before moving to Copenhagen as a member of the Royal Theatre Orchestra. By the time he died Nielsen's symphonies and operas had made him world famous. As well as the museum to the composer in Odense, there is one in his birthplace at Årslev about 12km (7.5 miles) southeast of the city.

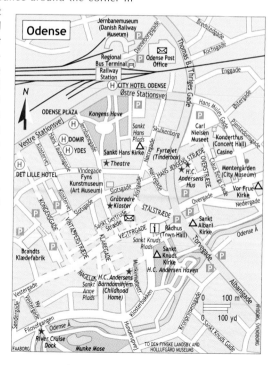

Below: *Odense's Rådhus (Town Hall) which stands in a pedestrianized square across from the cathedral.*

HC Andersens Hus, where the writer is said to have been born in 1805. Andersen was the son of an impoverished cobbler and a washerwoman who soon moved to an even smaller house. Andersen's father died when he was 11, and at 14 he left Odense (gratefully, as his had been a miserable childhood) hoping to become an actor in Copenhagen. He had one role, a walk-on as a troll. But his writing was a success and from early poems and stories his world-famous fairy tales developed. *The Little Mermaid*, *The Ugly Duckling* and others have now been translated into 170 languages and Andersen is claimed to be the world's most read author. One tale, *The Nightingale*, was dedicated to Jenny Lind, the 'Swedish Nightingale', with whom Andersen fell in (unrequited) love. The sexually ambiguous Andersen was a tortured soul. After almost dying in a hotel fire, he always travelled with a length of rope so that he could escape from a window. He wanted to be taken seriously as a writer, but it was children's stories that made him famous. He died wealthy, but unhappy, in 1875. The house, protected by a steel portcullis emblazoned with a garish sun (the whole claimed by the museum management to 'harmonize' with the neighbouring houses) has a remarkable collection of memorabilia (open mid-Jun to mid-Aug daily 09:00–18:00; mid-Aug to mid-Jun Tue–Sun 10:00–16:00). There is a statue of Andersen in the marvellous park behind the cathedral, while his **childhood home** (in Munkemøllestræde) is another museum to him (open mid-Jun to mid-Aug daily 10:00–16:00; mid-Aug to mid-Jun Tue–Sun 11:00–15:00).

From the delightful streets close to HC Andersens Hus, head south to Overgade which has some beautiful buildings. No 48 is **Møntergården**, the city museum (open Tue–Sun 10:00–16:00). Also close to HC Andersens Hus is the Odense **casino** and **concert hall**, the latter including a museum to the city's other famous son, Carl Nielsen (open Jan–Aug Thu and Fri 14:00–18:00, Sun 12:00–16:00; Sep–May Thu and Fri 16:00–20:00, Sun 12:00–16:00). To the west of Flakhaven, **Brandts Klæde-fabrik** is an old textile mill which has been converted into a centre with several fine museums including one on printing, another of

photography, and a fine art gallery (open Tue–Sun 10:00–17:00, also open Mon in Jul and Aug). There is another excellent art museum – **Fyns Kunstmuseum** – to the north of the city centre (open Tue–Sun 10:00–16:00). Railway enthusiasts will be more interested in the nearby **Jernbanemuseum**, the Danish Railway Museum, which has not only a collection for adults, but also mini-trains for children to enjoy (open daily 10:00–16:00). To complete the cultural picture, the **Hollufgård** is a museum of prehistory (open Apr–Oct Thu–Sun 10:00–16:00; Nov–Mar Sun only), while to the south of the city **Den Fynske Landsby** is an open-air museum of life in 19th-century Fyn, with a reconstructed village around a duck pond (open mid-Jun to mid-Aug daily 09:30–19:00; Apr to mid-June and mid-Aug to Oct Tue–Sun 10:00–17:00; Nov–Mar Sun 11:00–15:00).

Above: *Den Gamle Kro (The Old Inn), one of the best and most atmospheric restaurants in Odense.*

WEST FYN *

Middelfart is named for its central position at the narrowest crossing of the Little Belt. The position made it an ideal ferry point, bringing prosperity but also making it a target in time of war. Both aspects are explored in the Town Museum. The town also has a fine ceramics museum (open all year Tue–Sun 11:00–17:00). Close to

THANK YOU VERY MUCH

Though not listed in the brochure of Odense's museums, the city has a museum to a dead king (as well as the remains of a murdered one). In the basement of the superbowl in Grønløkken (to the west of the Flakhaven) there is an Elvis Presley museum containing over 1000 items of memorabilia.

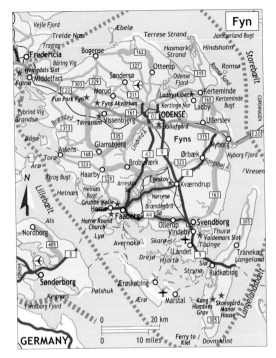

the old bridge the neo-classical **Hindsgavl Slot** is a conference centre, but the parkland around it is open to the public. There are spectacular views across the Little Belt to the tiny island of Fænø.

Inland from **Middelfart** there are a number of sites, all close to the E20 motorway, which will be of interest to families. **Fun Park Fyn** has rides and amusements including go-karts and terrific water slides. The **Fyns Akvarium** at Vissenbjerg has warm-water and saltwater tanks, while the nearby **Terrariet** is a reptile park contain-ing snakes and much else to frighten the willingly scared. **Lilleskov Teglværk**

Opposite: *The round church at Horne, best of its type outside Bornholm.*

is an old tile kiln, now a museum with miniature railway and trolley rides. Southeast of Middelfart is **Assens**, with a quaint old centre and harbour area. In the harbour is a statue of Peter Willemoes (1783–1808) who died a hero in the battle of Sjællands Odde in 1808 (*see* panel, page 103). He stands close to a cooking house, a reminder of the days when sailors were not allowed fires on board wooden ships in the harbour and had to cook on shore.

North of the E20 there is fine country dotted with pretty villages. The biggest is **Bogense**, where visitors will be astonished to see a replica of the Brussels *Mannekin Pis* as well as several old and beautiful buildings. Those wanting to improve on their astonishment level could try the Museum of Potatoes at **Otterup** to the east, with picking machines, grading machines and the story of how the potato influenced the cultural development of north Fyn.

South Fyn ***

From Odense, road No. 43 heads south to **Faaborg**, a
fascinating town that is an open-air gallery of Danish
sculptural art. The tight streets around Torvet (the central
square) are very picturesque, as is the elegant Vesterport,
a 15th-century brick town gate, which spans Vestergade.
It is one of very few gates remaining in Danish towns. In
Torvet stands Kai Nielsen's controversial work,
Ymerbrønden. There is another Nielsen statue in the
town, as well as other fine works (a guide leaflet is available from the Tourist Office by the sea). There is more
quality art (and the original *Ymerbrønden*) in the **Town
Museum** (open Apr–Oct daily 10:00–16:00; Nov–Mar
Tue–Sun 11:00–15:00). The town's other museum, in
Den Gamle Gård, is an 18th-century half-timbered merchant's house with interesting collections of furniture,
toys and much more (open mid-May to mid-Sep daily
10:30–16:30; Apr to mid-May, mid-Sep to Oct Sat and
Sun 11:00–15:00). One curio is a lock of HC Andersen's
hair given to Riborg Voigt, a local merchant's daughter
who befriended the writer.

West of Faaborg, **Grubbe Mølle** is a refurbished
windmill and watermill, both now functional (open July,
daily tour at 11:00). Nearby, at **Horne**, stands the only
round church on Fyn (and one of only seven in
Denmark). Unfortunately the church was later extended,
and both a nave and a huge west front were added. The
result looks somewhat odd, since the new sections
detract from the original.

YMERBRØNDEN

In Norse mythology Ymer was
a giant created from
the water drops that fell from
the frozen north. He was fed
by the milk of the cow
Audhumle which was created
from the same drops. Later
Audhumle, while licking a
glacier for moisture, exposed
the father of the Norse gods.
The gods were afraid of Ymer
and killed him, his blood creating the rivers and oceans, his
bones the cliffs at the water's
edge. Kai Nielsen's statue
shows Audhumle feeding
Ymer, the god child. The statue
caused a sensation when first
revealed as it was deemed
indecent. The statue now
standing in Faaborg's Torvet is
a bronze replica of the soap-
stone original which was
being eroded away by the
weather.

ÆBELØ

Lying off the north Fyn coast is
Æbelø, named for the crab
apple trees which grow there.
Once home to a farming
community, the population
dwindled away in the face of
harsh winters and the pleasures
of the mainland. Today the
island is left to the wildlife –
insects especially, but also roe
deer and mouflon – and the
plants. Visitors must be both
intrepid and able to read a
tidetable as the only approach
is wading at low tide.

From Faaborg, road No. 8 heads northeast through beautiful rolling country (somewhat hopefully called the Fyn Alps by the local tourist offices) to reach **Egeskov**, the most magical castle in Denmark, complete with moat and drawbridge. The castle was built in the mid-16th century on oak piles driven into the centre of an existing pond, the construction giving it its name, *egeskov* – oak wood. The medieval fortress was restored in the 19th century as a stately home. The castle is worth visiting for its furnishings, weapons and artwork. But the castle is only one of a kaleidoscope of treasures, including museums of veteran cars (above which old aircraft are suspended), old motorcycles and horse-drawn carriages, several mazes, and rose, herbaceous and water gardens, amongst many others, these spread among the beautiful parkland that surrounds the castle. For children, apart from the mazes there are playgrounds, Dracula's crypt and the tree-top walk (open May and Sep daily 10:00–17:00; Jun and Aug daily 10:00–18:00; Jul daily 10:00–20:00; the castle closes one hour earlier in Jun–Aug).

Continuing northeast the visitor passes more delightful country to reach **Ørbæk**. Close to this neat village are some of Denmark's most important prehistoric sites, such as the Lindeskov dolmen (*see* page 12).

THE FYN ISLANDS **

At Fyn's southeastern corner lies **Svendborg**, an industrial town with some picturesque buildings at its old heart. Viebæltegård, the old almshouse, is now an archaeological museum, while the 16th-century half-timbered Anne Hvides Gård is a local history museum. From Svendborg a road crosses to the island of Tåsinge from which you reach Langeland, while a ferry crosses to Ærø.

Tåsinge was the site of Denmark's most tragic love affair, that between Sixten

Sparre, a Swedish Count, and Hedvig Jensen, a tightrope dancer who used the stage name Elvira Madigan. When their romance was doomed – by social convention or by her reluctance – Sparre shot her and then himself. Whether this was murder and suicide or double suicide is not clear. The two are buried at **Landet Kirke**.

Less gloomy is **Valdemars Slot**, a 17th-century Baroque castle, beautifully sited and furnished in opulent style (open May–Sep daily 10:00–17:00 (Tue 10:00–18:00); closed Mon in Sep). The castle includes an impressive Toy Museum with a history of toys dating back to the 19th century.

From Tåsinge a causeway crosses to Siø and on to **Langeland**, a popular resort island – its beaches are safe for children. **Rudkøbing**, the 'capital', has some pretty streets and a statue of Hans Christian Ørsted, the town's most famous son. To the north, at **Tranekær**, a 13th-century castle stands beside a lake. The surrounding parkland has several environmental works by international artists, and also a small arboretum (open June to Oct Mon–Fri 10:00–17:00, Sun 13:00–17:00). South of Rudkøbing, **Skovsgård** Manor House is the centrepiece of a conservation and organic farming project (open Apr–Oct daily 10:00–17:00). Further south, **Kong Humbles Grav** is Denmark's largest Stone-Age burial chamber, while the southern tip of Langeland is popular with bird-watchers.

Ærø is the destination for those who want peace and quiet, the popular way to explore it being by bicycle. The thatched cottages and windmills are charming and there are several prehistoric sites to explore.

NYBORG AND EAST FYN **

Too often visitors flash past **Nyborg** heading to, or from, the Great Belt Bridge, but this lovely little town repays the effort of its exploration. Nyborg, the new castle, was built in the 12th century as one of several fortresses protecting Fyn from marauding Wends. The castle was a royal palace for centuries, but during the Swedish war of

Above: *The motor and aircraft museum, one of many delights at Egeskov Castle.*

Opposite: *With its moat, entrance bridge and conical tower tops, Egeskov can hardly be bettered by the fairy-tale castles of a Hans Christian Andersen story.*

THE MAGNETIC PROF ØRSTED

Hans Christian Ørsted (1777–1851) was born in Rudkøbing, the son of the town apothecary. He had no formal education, but easily passed the Copenhagen University entrance examination. He became the university's Professor of Physics and in 1820 discovered the magnetic effect of an electric current, a discovery which led to the work of Michael Faraday. Ørsted, a good friend of HC Andersen, has given his name to the unit of magnetic field strength (the Oersted chosen to avoid the use of Ø).

Above: *Away from the famous castle, Nyborg has other delights such as its excellent harbour.*

1658 it was partially destroyed. Its outer defensive rampart was torn down to allow the town to expand and, when finally rescued for posterity, only a section of the original building remained. Now stabilized, it is open to the public and worth visiting for its collection of armour and weapons (open Jul daily 10:00–17:00; Jun and Aug daily 10:00–16:00; May and Sep daily 10:00–15:00). The town is also worth exploring, particularly Slotsgade beside the lake/moat, and the main square and the pedestrianized streets that lead from it. Mads Lerches Gåde, set where Slotsgade joins Kangegade, is the town's oldest house, dating from 1601. It is now the town museum (opening times as for the castle). On Gammel Torv, the church dates from the 14th century and has a superb Baroque pulpit carved by Anders Mortensen, an Odense master.

North of Nyborg, **Kerteminde** is a pleasant seaside town with a museum to Johannes Larsen, a local wildlife and landscape painter. Larsen probably drew inspiration from **Romsø**, an island to the north which has a deer herd and excellent bird life. Close to the town, Fjord & Baelt – Go Under Water – has huge pools with porpoises and seals. There are underwater tunnels for viewing close up at regular feeding times as well as shows. Open daily mid-Jun to mid-Aug 10:00–16:00. Weekends from mid-Feb to Nov, at the same times. West of Kerteminde, at **Ladby**, the ship-tomb of a 10th-century Viking has been excavated, the only one of its kind so far discovered in Denmark. Although almost nothing but the ship outline remains, the site is very atmospheric (open Jun–Aug daily 10:00–16:00; Sep, Oct and Mar–May Tue–Sun 10:00–16:00; Nov–Feb Wed–Sun 11:00–15:00).

BRIDGING THE GREAT BELT

The 18km (11-mile) Great Belt Bridge comprises a motorway and railway track. The 6.6km (4.1-mile) West Bridge (Nyborg to Sprogø Island) was completed in 1993. The East Bridge, 6.8km (4.3 miles), which has a free span of 1624m (1776yd), was completed in 1998. The 254m (833ft) towers of the East Bridge are the tallest structures in Scandinavia. The railway was opened in 1997 and is Europe's second longest tunnel, sinking to 75m (246ft) below the sea bed. The whole project took 66,000 man years of effort to complete.

Fyn at a Glance

BEST TIMES TO VISIT

Summer is most popular and has the advantage of long days to explore the countryside. Spring and autumn are also very good: Fyn is a fertile island, those times adding colour to splendid scenery. Winter can be cold and windy.

GETTING THERE

The airport at Odense connects with Copenhagen. A railway line crosses the island (utilizing the new Belt bridges), as does the E20 motorway. Fyn's road system is excellent, particularly in the south of the island.

GETTING AROUND

Reasonable bus service between the bigger towns, but the service to outlying villages is limited. A railway links Odense and Svendborg.

WHERE TO STAY

There are good hotels all over Fyn, particularly in Odense.

LUXURY
Clarion Odense Plaza Hotel, Østre Stationsvej 24, 5000 Odense C, tel: 66 117745, fax: 66 144145. Close to railway station and a short way from the main sights. Old hotel, now a member of the Best Western chain. Good facilities.
Slotpension Valdemars Slot, Slotsalléen 100, 5700 Tåsinge, tel: 62 225900, fax: 62 227267. Live like a king in a wing of the castle. Four-poster beds add to the splendour.

MID-RANGE
City Hotel Odense, Overgade 23, 5000 Odense C, tel: 66 121258, fax: 66 129364. Across the road from the casino and so within a few minutes walk of all the main sights. Very clean and bright.
Hotel Faaborg Fjord, Svendborgvej 175, 5600 Faaborg, tel: 62 611010, fax: 63 606160. Part of the Quality hotel chain. On the eastern edge of the town, but still within walking distance of the centre. Excellent facilities and restaurant.

BUDGET
Hotel Domir, Hans Tausens Gade 19, 5000 Odense C, tel: 66 121427, fax: 66 121413. Very reasonably priced and includes a good breakfast. Close to the railway station.

WHERE TO EAT

All the main towns and villages have fine restaurants, but one deserves a special mention:
Den Gamle Kro, Overgade 23, 5000 Odense C, tel: 66 121433, fax: 66 178858. The old inn, now a fine restaurant; traditional Danish cooking in superb surroundings. Not cheap, but outstanding.

SHOPPING

Odense is excellent for shopping. Magasin is a large departmental store in Vestergade, while the Rosengårdcentret in Odense SØ (southeast of the centre) is not only the largest shopping mall on Fyn, but in Denmark. Nyborg and Svendborg both have good shopping centres while most of the smaller towns and villages have craft outlets.

TOURS AND EXCURSIONS

The Tourist Information Offices have details of sightseeing tours and excursions. Odense offers a city tour.

USEFUL CONTACTS

Tourist Information Offices:
Banegårdspladsen 2a, 5600 Faaborg, tel: 62 610707, fax: 62 613337;
Torvet 9, 5800 Nyborg, tel: 65 310280, fax: 65 310380;
Rådhuset, 5000 Odense C, tel: 66 127520, fax: 66 127586;
Torvet 5, 5900 Rudkøbing, Langeland, tel: 62 513505, fax: 62 514335;
Centrumpladsen 4, 5700 Svendborg, tel: 62 210980, fax: 62 220553.

ODENSE	J	F	M	A	M	J	J	A	S	O	N	D
AVERAGE TEMP. °C	0	0	2	7	12	15	17	16	13	9	5	2
AVERAGE TEMP. °F	32	32	36	45	54	59	63	61	55	48	41	36
RAINFALL mm	49	35	30	35	39	46	64	80	56	63	49	46
RAINFALL in	1.9	1.4	1.2	1.4	1.5	1.8	2.5	3.2	2.2	2.5	1.9	1.8

6
Zealand

Because Copenhagen lies on Zealand it has become the natural home for many Danish institutions which enhance the attractiveness of an island already popular with visitors. Yet for all that the northeast corner, around Copenhagen, is home to a quarter of all Danes and so is heavily urbanized, much of Zealand is still essentially rural while the adjacent islands of **Lolland**, **Falster** and **Møn**, to the south, are as peaceful and secluded as anywhere in north Jutland – and every bit as scenic.

But it is the famous names which draw the crowds: **Roskilde** with its cathedral, burial place of Danish rulers, and its Viking ship museum; and **Helsingør**, famous for Hamlet's castle (even if the prince is entirely a figment of Shakespeare's imagination). In **Rungsted** is the home of Karen Blixen, her fame as a writer now eclipsed by that created by the film *Out of Africa*. To these can be added more recent art galleries whose architecture makes them as worth visiting as the works they contain: **Louisiana** to the north of Copenhagen and **Arken** to the south. Add a sprinkling of royal castles and beautiful old towns, stir in the stunning scenery of **Møn** and **Stevns Klint**, and add the possibility of a quick visit to Sweden by ferry from Helsingør, or across the new Øresund bridge, and it can be readily seen that Zealand has something for everyone.

These delights are within easy reach of Copenhagen, and the city makes an ideal base to tour the island. Trains connect many of the more interesting towns, while the new motorway system means that few Zealand towns are now more than an hour or so from the capital.

DON'T MISS

*** Roskilde: the only preserved Viking ships in Denmark – and they are still being made.
*** Louisiana: quite stunning new art gallery.
** Frederiksborg Castle: beautiful castle and gardens.
** Helsingør: Hamlet's castle and an attractive little town.
** Møn and **Stevns Klint:** some of the most impressive coastal scenery in Denmark.
** Trelleborg: reconstructed Viking fort and longhouse.
* Rungsted: enjoy Karen Blixen's house and parkland.

Opposite: *The Little Heddinge windmill in southern Zealand.*

CLIMATE

Zealand is drier and cooler than the rest of Denmark, the sheltering effect of Fyn and Jutland being seen in the rainfall figures, the nearness of the Baltic and Russia in the temperature data. As elsewhere in the country the best time to visit is **summer**, but since many of Denmark's top tourist sites (and Copenhagen) are on Zealand, and as most are indoors, any time of year is good.

THE VIKINGS AT HOME

North of Korsør, Trelleborg is another of the four ring fortresses built by Harald Bluetooth, and as with Fyrkat on Jutland it has been renovated and has a reconstructed Viking longhouse to help visitors to catch a glimpse of Viking life. In summer the site staff dress in Viking clothes and give exhibitions of Viking crafts, these and the site museum with its artefacts bringing Trelleborg alive. The site is also quite remote, the drive to it probably giving some idea of how Viking Denmark looked.

LOCH NESS

Close to Kalundborg, Loch Ness is excellent for birdwatchers. There is a play area for children but the lake seems to lack a monster.

WEST ZEALAND ★★

Before the opening of the Great Belt Bridge the ferries linking Fyn and Zealand travelled between Nyborg and Korsør. Today visitors on the motorway tend to hurry past the town, missing both it and Zealand's west coast sites. One that lies close to the first exit of the motorway, just beyond the toll booths, is the drill head used to bore the Belt tunnels. It lies in the grass rusting and forlorn, but still impressively large. In a neat twist, moles, nature's own tunnellers, have made their hills around it.

In **Korsør** the Fæstning is one of very few medieval fortress towers remaining in Denmark. Built in the 13th century to defend the harbour entrance, it is now a local history museum. In the town centre Kongegården, King's courtyard, an 18th-century rococo house, was where royalty ate as they waited for the ferry (or the weather). It is now a cultural centre and is located in a very picturesque area.

South of Korsør, **Skælskør** is a charming port, the surrounding area popular with bird-watchers and day trippers crossing to the peaceful islands of **Agersø** and **Omø**. Inland of Korsør, **Slagelse** has an interesting craft museum (open mid-Jun to Sep Tue–Sun 13:00–17:00; Oct to mid-Jun Sat and Sun 13:00–17:00). **Sorø**, east of Slagelse, has interesting monastic remains, including the town church. The monastery was built by Bishop Absalon's father, Asser Rig, and Absalon is buried beneath the church's high altar. Sorø stands beside a lake and there are other lakes, most of them set in woodland, locally, making it one of the most scenically attractive areas on Zealand. At nearby **Bjernede** is Zealand's only round church.

North of Korsør is **Trelleborg**, the best of Denmark's Viking sites (daily 10:00–17:00). North again there is beautiful country peppered with pretty villages. **Tissø** is a lake popular with sailors, and close by there are opportunities for canoeing. **Reersø**, to the west, is one of Denmark's prettiest villages while **Kalundborg**, though industrial, is charmingly set around the 12th-century Vor Frue Kirke which, in ground plan, takes the form of a Greek cross.

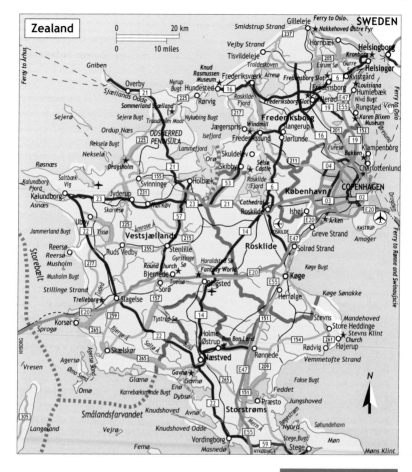

To the east, **Holbæk**, on the shore of Isefjord, has one of Europe's longest model railways and a whole collection of fine churches. Tuse church has an extraordinary 15th-century frescoed ceiling while Tveje Merløse, to the south of the town, is a miniature Roskilde cathedral.

Forming the western shore of Isefjord is the beautiful **Odsherred Peninsula**. This is an historically important area – the Bronze Age sun-chariot, now in the National Museum, was discovered on **Trundholm Moor**, an area

WINDMILLS

Modern windmills tap the power of the wind to provide the environmentally conscious Danes with 'green' electricity. In southern Zealand are the more traditional windmills, few of which are now used for their original purpose.

rich in prehistoric burial mounds. There is a copy of the chariot in **Høve** museum. The intrepid might like to stay in Dragsholm Castle, built in the 13th century and now a hotel. It is said to be haunted by three ghosts.

North of the moor, **Sommerland Sjælland** has the usual rides and play areas for children (open daily 10:00–17:00, later in summer).

History lovers will want to visit **Overby** on the unlikely **Sjællands Odde**, the narrow spit of land which pokes out at the north end of the peninsula, to see the memorials to the battle of 1808.

ROSKILDE ★★★

As early as the 10th century Harald Bluetooth realized the strategic importance of Roskilde, set on a cross-Zealand route and at the bottom of a deeply incut and sheltered fjord. Bluetooth is said to have built the first church here and it was here that he was buried. Nothing remains of Harald's church, though the foundations of the stone church that replaced it lie beneath Bishop Absalon's soaring brick cathedral. It is claimed that over 3 million bricks went into its construction, the use of brick on such a scale producing an edifice which seems to glow fire-red in setting sun.

As home to the most important church on Zealand, Roskilde prospered despite losing easy access to the sea after the events of the 11th century (see page 103). As

well as the cathedral there were two monasteries, three convents and several other churches here. But with the rise of Copenhagen and the closure of the monastic houses during the Reformation the town fell on hard times, and the cathedral's continuing use as a royal mausoleum was insufficient to stave off the decline. Today, with its visitor attractions and speedy rail connection to Copenhagen, Roskilde is once again reviving.

Since the Reformation all the Danish kings, and also most of their queens, have been buried in the **cathedral**. As several pre-Reformation kings were also interred here, that

makes a total of 39 kings and queens (37 definite burials, together with Harald Bluetooth and Svein Forkbeard who are believed to lie beneath the present building). Some of their tombs are splendid: that of Margrethe I (1375–1412) is outstanding. Elsewhere in the cathedral, be sure to see the superb altarpiece, made in Antwerp in 1560, and also look up on the north side of the nave to see the ornate, carved royal pew (open Apr–Sep Mon–Fri 09:00–16:45, Sat 09:00–12:00, Sun 12:30–16:45; Oct–Mar Tue–Sat 10:00–15:45, Sun 12:30–15:45).

Some time in the 11th century five longships were sunk at the mouth of Roskilde Fjord, and stones were piled on them to create a barrage that prevented marauders from using the fjord to reach the town. In 1962 the ships were salvaged and placed in a purpose-built museum. The ships represent the complete Viking range – raiders (the ship that struck fear into the hearts of men throughout northern Europe), ships for trade and those for passengers (the ships that transported the settlers of new lands). Together they form one of the great visitor sites of Denmark (open daily 10:00–17:00).

Recently the site has been enhanced by the addition of a boatyard and exhibition centre. Exact replicas of the Viking ships are being constructed, using original methods and tools, in the yard. Four of these have been completed and it is occasionally possible to take trips in them on Roskilde Fjord.

Above: *A detail of Queen Margrethe's tomb, the finest of the royal tombs in Roskilde Cathedral.*
Opposite: *The impressive Great Belt Bridge – a typically Danish mix of function and style.*

THE BATTLE OF SJÆLLANDS ODDE

In 1808 the *Prins Christian Frederik*, the pride of the Danish Navy, was sunk by a British squadron in a battle off this narrow spit of land. The hero of the battle was Peter Willemoes, whose statue can be seen in Assens (*see page 92*). Willemoes was one of the 64 Danish sailors killed. There is a model of the Danish ship in Overby church where the names of the dead, who were buried in a mass grave, are inscribed on panels. The memorial column is by Vilhelm Bissen, a pupil of Bertel Thorvaldsen.

Above: *One of Europe's great survivals: the Viking ships of Roskilde.*
Opposite: *Knud Rasmussen – half-Dane, half-Greenlander – was one of the greatest Arctic explorers of the 20th century.*

The main Roskilde **museum** explores the history of the town (open daily 11:00–16:00). Another part, just a short step away, takes the form of an early 20th-century grocery. Next door is a **museum of old tools** (open Mon–Fri 07:00–16:30, Sun 08:00–12:30). The town also has an interesting **museum of contemporary art** (open Tue–Fri 11:00–17:00, Sun–Mon 12:00–16:00).

NORTHEAST ZEALAND ★★★

North of Roskilde a fjord-side road heads north towards Frederikssund, passing through **Jørlunde** where the frescoed church was built by members of Bishop Absalon's family. **Slangerup**, the next town, is a very old place, once an important stop on the road from Roskilde to Helsingør. Denmark's first convent was built here by King Valdemar I. **Frederikssund** is a charming place set at the narrowest point of Roskilde Fjord. The town's Viking settlement seeks to recreate local life in Viking times (open daily 09:00–17:00), while the JF Williamsens Museum displays the painting and sculpture of the symbolist who is now regarded as one of Denmark's leading 20th-century artists (open Tue–Sun 10:00–17:00). Williamsens gave his collection to the

THE VIKING PLAYS

Each year for two weeks in late June or early July a series of plays presenting Viking traditions and legends are presented at an open-air theatre in Frederikssund, sometimes with casts of up to 200. Visitors can also join in an 'authentic' Viking banquet after each play.

town, but did not live to see the museum opened. He is buried in the nearby park. Across the bridge which spans the fjord, the Færgegården Museum explores the history of Frederikssund and the Jægerspris Peninsula (open Jun–Aug Tue–Sun 10:00–16:00; Mar–May and Sep–Dec Tue–Fri 10:00–16:00).

Jægerspris has a fine old windmill, struck by lightning in 2002 but hopefully soon restored, and an impressive castle. Dating from the 14th century, it was given by King Frederik VII to his wife. She had been born Louise Rasmussen, a commoner, and though made Countess Danner, was never made queen or accepted by the aristocracy. The Countess established a home for 'help-less and deserted young ladies, more especially those of humble origins' at the castle, the title suggesting more than a hint of sweet revenge. The Countess demanded to be buried in an open mound – her sarcophagus can still be seen (open Easter to Oct Tue–Sun 11:00–15:00).

South of Jægerspris, **Skuldelev** is where the ships displayed in Roskilde were found. The town has a fascinating museum of toys and dolls (open mid-Jun to mid-Aug daily 10:00–16:00; Mar to mid-Jun and mid-Aug to Oct Tue and Thu 10:00–15:00, Sun 10:00–16:00). South again, Selsø Castle, near **Skibby**, dates from the 16th century (though it replaced an earlier building). It has collections of weapons and armour, model ships and costumes, but is chiefly interesting for its furnishings (open Jun–Oct daily 11:00–16:00). The nearby lake, once an inlet of the fjord, is a bird sanctuary.

North of Frederikssund is **Frederiksværk**, its name easily mis-taken, but quite different. It lays claim to being Denmark's oldest industrial town, having been created around a cannon foundry and gun-

KNUD RASMUSSEN

Half-Danish, half-Greenlandic, Knud Rasmussen (1879–1933) was born in Greenland and is famous for his series of 'Thule' expeditions, often in the company of his Danish friend and co-worker Peter Freuchen. The Thule expeditions pieced together the history and culture of the Inuit folk of the Arctic, as well as filling in details on the map of northern Greenland. During the Fifth Thule Expedition, the most famous, Rasmussen completed a transit of the Northwest Passage by dog-sledge in winter. He died of food poisoning brought on by eating tainted pickled puffin.

HOLGER THE DANE

In the dungeon of Kronborg Castle is a stone statue of Holger Danske who, legend has it, is only sleeping, but will awake to save Denmark in its hour of need.

FREDERIKSBORG CHAPEL

The once private royal chapel of Frederiksborg Castle is now the Hillerød town church. It escaped the disastrous fire of 1859, which means King Christian IV's ostentatious style can be seen at first hand. Of the treasures, the greatest are the altar and pulpit by Jakob Mores, a Hamburg goldsmith, and the 16th-century Compensius organ which has 1000 pipes. This is played at 13:30 on Thursdays.

Below: *A ferry leaves Helsingør for the short journey across Øresund to Helsingborg in Sweden.*

powder mill by King Frederik V in 1756. The works were powered by water from a canal dug between Arresø lake and the fjord. Today the wooded shores of the lake are ideal for walks and picnics. The town's industrial history is depicted in the Bymuseum and gunpowder mill museum (open Jun to mid-Sep Tue–Sun 12:00–16:00). There is also a fire brigade museum – given the work carried out in the town, that is really no surprise (open Jun–Sep Sat 10:00–14:00). From the town the main road leads to **Hundested** at the mouth of the fjord, from where a ferry crosses to Rørvig. Hundested, named for the seals which can still be seen offshore, is famous as the home of Knud Rasmussen, Denmark's most famous polar explorer. His house is a museum to the man and his expeditions (open Apr–Oct Tue–Sun 11:00–16:00).

The northern coast of Zealand has some very pleasant seaside towns. **Tisvildeleje** is a good centre for walking, both on the coast and in Troldeskoven (witch wood – named for the eerie look of the wind-battered trees) to the south. **Gilleleje** has a fishing harbour and more excellent coastal walks – make for the Nakkehoved Østre Fyr lighthouse, now restored as a museum (open Jun–Aug Wed–Mon 13:00–16:00 and Sep–May Wed and Fri 13:00–16:00, Thu 13:00–18:00, Sun 10:00–14:00). **Hornbæk**, to the east, has the best of all north Zealand beaches: white sand backed by dunes topped with pink roses. There are also excellent walks in the woodland that extends east from the town. Next is **Helsingør** which is

more than a seaside resort; most visitors come here to enjoy the vast **Kronborg Castle**. Situated at the narrowest point of Øresund, the strategic importance of the site was obvious from earliest times. King Erik built a fort in the 1420s, but the present building was erected by Frederik II in 1577 as a way of impos-

Above: *Kronborg Castle, model for Shakespeare's Elsinore and home to one of Europe's best maritime museums.*

ing his right to collect fees from ships passing through the narrows. In 1658 the castle was occupied and stripped bare by the Swedes. It then became a barracks, but in 1923 it was restored to its medieval glory and opened to the public. A museum in its own right, it also houses the Danish Maritime Museum (open May–Sep daily 10:30–17:00; Apr and Oct Tue–Sun 11:00–16:00; Nov–Mar Tue–Sun 11:00–15:00). The town itself is also worth exploring. It has a wealth of quaint streets and places, and a remarkable number of attractions – wine, history and traffic/aviation museums, Denmark's Technical Museum of Science and Technology, an aquarium, and an old steam train that trundles along the north coast to Hornbæk and Gilleleje. It is also possible to hop on a ferry for a day trip to Helsingborg in Sweden.

Inland from Helsingør the visitor can overdose on castles. Take road No. 6, passing **Kvistgård**, where there is an excellent toy museum, to reach **Fredensborg Slot** (Peace Castle), built in 1720 and named to commemorate the end of another war with Sweden. The castle, in elegant understated Baroque style, is now the summer home of the royal family. When Queen Margrethe is in residence the guard changes every day. If the Queen is not in residence the castle is occasionally open to the public. The magnificent wooded parkland surrounding the castle is open and includes an amphitheatre with about 70 life-sized statues of Danish folk – fishermen, farmers, etc. – in traditional dress.

SHAKESPEARE'S HAMLET

Though it is extremely unlikely that Shakespeare ever visited Kronborg Castle it is likely he had heard of it, news of so majestic and important a place travelling quickly across Europe. There is no historical basis for the play, though versions of the tale had been in circulation since the 12th century when it appeared in the *Historia Danica*, that version dealing with a mythical Danish King and giving Shakespeare his idea for setting his work in Elsinore (the Anglicized version of Helsingør). Hamlet did, however, include two real Danes, Rosencrantz and Guildenstern being based on Frederik Rosenkrantz and Knud Gyldenstierne who visited the English court in the 1590s.

Above: *The breathtakingly ornate Great Hall of Frederiksborg Castle.*

Further on, at **Hillerød**, is a very different kind of castle. **Frederiksborg Slot** – not to be confused with Copenhagen's Frederiksberg Slot – is anything but understated; it is a stupendous red-brick castle in Dutch Renaissance style, set on islands in a lake beyond which there are both Baroque and English gardens. King Frederik II built the palatial castle as a summer residence in 1560, though what we see now is largely the work of his son, Christian IV, whose style could most charitably be called extravagant. The castle was gutted by fire in 1859 but was saved from total ruin by the Carlsberg beer magnate JC Jacobsen and is now a national treasure house of art and furnishings (open mid-Mar to Oct daily 10:00–17:00; Nov–Mar daily 11:00–15:00).

Following the coast road south from Helsingør the visitor reaches **Louisiana** to the left. This gallery of modern art is set in idyllic surroundings, some works being outdoors in the grounds which slope towards the sea. The grounds alone make a visit worthwhile, but the art makes the day complete – a stunning permanent collection of contemporary work by both Danish and European artists as well as temporary exhibitions by modern masters. The artists to be seen at Louisiana include Picasso, Henry Moore, Joan Miró, Andy Warhol and Max Ernst. Other galleries may boast more expensive collections, but few can match the surroundings (open daily 10:00–17:00, but until 22:00 on Wed).

Continuing along the coast past Humlebæk the visitor reaches **Rungsted** and, opposite the marina, the **Karen Blixen Museum**. Karen Blixen (1885–1962) was born Karen Dinesen (which explains her pseudonym

WHY LOUISIANA?

The curious name of the modern art gallery derives from the three owners of the site previous to the museum. All of them had wives called Louise, a strange coincidence and one thought too good to be ignored.

Isak Dinesen) in Rungsted to well-to-do parents and studied art in Copenhagen, Rome and Paris. In 1914, after a failed love affair with his twin brother Hans, she married her second cousin Baron Bror von Blixen-Finecke. He wanted her money, she wanted his title. The couple moved to a Kenyan coffee farm where the Baron made Karen's life a misery with his womanizing: he also gave her syphilis. She consoled herself with an affair with Denys Finch Hatton, an upper-crust English pilot and big-game hunter. Their relationship was the basis of *Out of Africa*, the Oscar-winning film. Karen divorced her husband, but when Hatton died in an air crash she returned to Rungsted. She remained there until her death. Her writing was in English and only translated into Danish after achieving success and critical acclaim in the USA. The Danes did not initially take to her, finding her snobbish depiction of an aristocratic tier of society at odds with the society they were trying to create. They also disliked the fact that she referred to herself as Baroness. Today she is seen as a literary giant and her influence on modern Danish writers is readily acknowledged. Though *Out of Africa* is Blixen's most famous work, *Seven Gothic Tales* is her critical masterpiece. An adaptation of her story *Babette's Feast* won the Oscar for Best Foreign Film in 1987. Her home in Rungsted is now a museum to her (open May–Sep Tue–Sun 10:00–17:00; Oct–Apr Wed–Fri 13:00–16:00, Sat and Sun 11:00–16:00).

South again, just before Copenhagen is reached, the **Bakken** park at **Klampenborg** will keep children entertained for hours with its rides and shows (open Easter to mid-Sep Mon–Fri 14:00–00:00, Sat and Sun 13:00–00:00).

> **RUNGSTEDLUND**
>
> Rungstedlund (Rungsted Grove) once an inn, was bought by Karen Blixen's father and is where she grew up and lived until her death. While there Karen set up a foundation which manages the estate for its plants and bird life. The house is now a museum to her and includes some of her own paintings as well as the usual memorabilia. The writer is buried beneath a beech tree near the base of Ewald's Hill, named for the poet Johanses Ewald who lived at the old inn.

Below: *Some of the exhibits at Louisiana are outdoors, on lush lawns overlooking Øresund.*

THE BATTLE OF KØGE BAY

In 1677 the Swedish navy was thwarted in its invasion ambitions by defeat at the hands of Admiral Niels Juel in a battle in Køge Bay. Juel has become one of the heroes of Denmark for his tactics and bravery, but the battle has produced one distortion of history. Despite what the National Anthem says, King Christian V did not oversee the battle from the top of 'the lofty mast of his flagship' but from the top of Køge church tower.

Opposite: *The pulpit of Højerup Church, a building now severely undermined by collapse of the chalk cliffs on which it stands.*
Below: *The Arken, the modern art gallery south of Copenhagen; the design is as avant-garde as the works it contains.*

SOUTH ZEALAND ★★

Though northeast Zealand has the major visitor attractions and offers the most worthwhile trips from Copenhagen, this part of the island should not be ignored. It offers a peaceful alternative to the bustle of the more popular spots, and one or two pleasant surprises. 'Peaceful alternative' is not the first phrase that comes to mind for the visitor driving down the coast road (rather than the E47/E55) from the capital if a weekend day has been chosen for the drive. Then, it seems, the entire population of Copenhagen has had the same idea. The first worthwhile place is **Arken** (The Ark), a new contemporary art museum at **Ishøj**. Unfortunately the car park for the museum is also the car park for the beach, so if the weather is good, come on a weekday or come by train. The concrete and glass building was the work of 25-year-old architect Søren Robert Lund in 1996. It was, and remains, controversial. What is not in doubt is that it has been neglected and is showing signs of age, despite its youth. The art collection is chiefly Danish and is as surprising as it should be.

Further to the south, **Køge** is a lovely town, one of Denmark's best medieval survivals, now nicely enhanced by modern art works. To enjoy the best of old Køge, follow Nørregade north from the Torvet. Just

before the Skitsesamling (the museum of art sketches – preliminary sketches for public art works – open Tue–Sun 10:00–17:00), turn left along Katekismusgade, then turn left again into Kirkestræde to return to Torvet. A number of the half-timbered houses in Kirkestræde date from the late 16th and early 17th centuries. In Torvet, look for the plaque on No. 2 (at the corner of Nørregade) marked *Kiøge Huskors* (Kiøge being an old spelling of Køge: the translation is Køge Evil Cross). This commemorates an incident in 1612 in which some residents were accused of witchcraft, several being burned at the stake. In Nørregade a superb 16th-century half-timbered house is now the town museum (open Jun–Aug Tue–Sun 11:00–17:00; Sep–May Tue–Fri and Sun 13:00–17:00, Sat 11:00–15:00). The town also has a toy museum (open Danish school holidays, Fri and Sat 11:00–16:00) and a model village (how Køge looked in 1865 at 1:10 scale – open Jun–Aug Mon–Fri 10:00–16:00, Sat and Sun 11:00–15:00; May and Sep Mon–Fri 10:00–13:00).

Southeast of Køge, road No. 261 crosses **Stevns**, an area of pastoral beauty. At **Højerup** the old church is falling into the sea

as the dramatic chalk cliffs are eaten away. In the church, faded newspapers record the 1928 collapse. Beside the church, steep steps lead down to the sea for a close look at the cliffs. The perched church is an indication of the power of the sea to undermine the soft chalk. The drama of the church/cliff scene is at odds with the tranquillity of the village itself, prettily situated near a duck pond.

Inland of Køge, **Ringsted**, set right in the middle of Zealand, was an important market town in medieval times. This importance is reflected in Sankt Bendts Kirke, the burial place of several early kings of Denmark (including the first three Valdemars). During

HØJERUP OLD CHURCH

The old church was built in the 13th century and, legend has it, moves inland by one cock's stride each Christmas night. Sadly that movement has not been enough to avoid disaster. In 1928 the tower and part of the chancel collapsed into the sea. The church is now used only once each year (second Tuesday in August), a new church having been built.

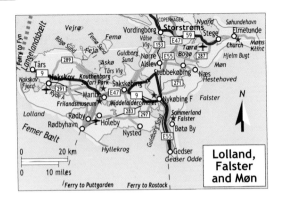

Lolland, Falster and Møn

the removal of the body of Queen Dagmar (wife of Valdemar II) to make way for another royal burial, the 11th-century Dagmar Cross, one of the National Museum's prized treasures, was discovered. Younger children will enjoy **Fantasy World,** near Ringsted, with its animated figures from HC Andersen's fairy tales (open Jun–Aug daily 10:00–17:00). Older children will prefer **Bon Bon Land** at **Holme-Østrup**, with its rides and slides (open May–Sep Mon–Fri 09:30–17:00, Sat, Sun and weekdays mid-Jun to mid-Aug 09:30–20:00; Sep–Oct Sat and Sun 09:30–17:00). Holme-Østrup is close to **Næstved** which has several interesting churches and a museum housed in what was the 14th-century hospital and poor house. One part of the museum (in Sankt Peders Kirkeplads) is a row of reconstructed medieval craftsmen's shops dating from the early 15th century. The shops are Denmark's oldest example of a terraced building and now house a collection of local glassware and ceramics (open Tue–Sun 10:00–16:00). Glassware is still made in the town, and the Holmegaard Glasværke is open to visitors who wish to watch the process (and buy the product). While looking around Næstved, be sure to take in the statues. The town has what it claims is Denmark's small equestrian statue (in Hjultorv) and also a troll (Teatergade) who looks surprisingly like a (naked) cricketing fast bowler.

At nearby **Gavnø** the rococo castle has magnificent gardens and a greenhouse with free-flying tropical butterflies (open mid-Apr to May daily 10:00–17:00, Jun–Sep daily 10:00–16:00, Oct–Dec daily 10:00–20:00).

LOLLAND, FALSTER AND MØN **

Lolland is the largest of the islands off Zealand's southern coast. At its west end ferries link **Tårs** with Langeland for those wanting a novel approach to Fyn. Nearby **Nakskov** is the island's largest town. Once a shipbuilding centre, it has now fallen on hard times. In the centre of the island is **Maribo**. In 1416 a convent of the order of St Bridget was set up here: Maribo Cathedral was the convent church and what little remains of the convent can be seen to the south. A painting of St Bridget – claimed to be the oldest painting on canvas in Scandinavia – is one of the cathedral's treasures. It is kept in a darkened room and access is limited. Close to the town the **Frilandsmuseum** is an open-air museum of old island buildings (open May–Sep daily 10:00–17:00). Also nearby is the **Knuthenborg Safari Park**. As well as the drive-through park there are beautiful gardens and a play area for children (open Easter to Sep daily 10:00–17:00). To the south of Maribo, at **Rødbyhavn**, ferries cross to the German island of Fehmarn. Eastwards, on the edge of the strait separating Lolland and Falster, is **Middelaldercentret** where craftworkers give demonstrations of medieval crafts. At certain times knights in armour joust, and a huge catapult is demonstrated (open May–Sep daily 10:00–16:00).

Nykøbing Falster – the name usually shortened to Nykøbing F – is Falster's capital (the F is required as Denmark has two other 'new markets'). Once heavily fortified against the Wends, all that remains of its castle is a model in the town museum. The museum is a fine half-timbered building in which Czar Peter the Great stayed in 1716. Close to the town is a good children's zoo with goats, monkeys and llamas (open Jun to mid-Apr daily 10:00–16:00; mid-Apr to Oct daily 09:00–18:00; Nov–Dec daily 10:00–16:00). Heading south from the capital, collectors of geographical memorabilia can reach **Gedser Odde**, the southernmost point of Denmark. The east coast of Falster is a popular holiday area, with camp sites and holiday homes.

ÅLHOLM SLOT

Near Nysted, at the south-eastern tip of Lolland, the 13th-century Ålholm castle is claimed to be the oldest inhabited castle in Europe. At one time the Danish King Christopher II was held prisoner in its dungeons by his half-brother, the somewhat inappropriately named Johan the Mild. The castle is not open to the public, but on the estate is a motor museum with around 200 veteran cars. A narrow-gauge railway can be used to explore the park around the castle.

MØNS KLINT

Not only are the chalk cliffs of Møns Klint wonderfully scenic, the area is also very good for walkers, who can descend to the beach below in several places, and amateur botanists. The chalk soil is excellent for flowers, with over 20 species of orchid growing on the grassy slopes including the delicate, beautiful dark red helleborine.

From **Stubbekøbing** a ferry crosses to the tiny island of Bogø, but the easier way to reach Møn is to take the E47/E55 motorway to Junction 42 (on an even tinier island, Farø) and then to cross Bogø.

Møn is by the far the most scenically attractive island, especially at its eastern end where **Møns Klint** is a series of impressive pure white chalk cliffs dropping into the Baltic's blue waters. The cliffs extend for over 10km (6 miles) and rise to a height of 128m (420ft) at the **Dronningenstol**, the Queen's Chair.

Møn is also famous for its frescoed churches, some of the finest in Denmark. The best are believed to have been painted by a single 15th-century artist, unknown apart from being referred to later as the Elmelunde Master. Not surprisingly his best work is in **Elmelunde** Church. The church also has a marvellous carved and painted altar. This, and the excellent pulpit, date from the 17th century. To see more by the Elmelunde Master, visit the churches at **Keldby** and **Fanefjord**.

Right: *The Danish sense of humour surfaces at this spot on the island of Lolland.*

Zealand at a Glance

BEST TIMES TO VISIT

Summer is the most popular. Spring and autumn are also very good, particularly in the south of the island and the offshore islands. Those wanting the best of Møn's flowers will certainly come in spring. Winter can be cold and windy.

GETTING THERE

Zealand can be reached by air. Railway lines cross the island east-west and north-south, the southern line continuing to Falster and Lolland. The E20 motorway gives access to the centre. The northeast is served by the E47/E55 (and road No. 16 which is motorway quality as far as Hillerød); that motorway also runs down the east coast to Falster and Lolland.

GETTING AROUND

There are excellent train and bus services from Copenhagen.

WHERE TO STAY

LUXURY

Hotel Prindsen, Algade 13, 4000 Roskilde, tel: 46 309100, fax: 46 309150. Best Western hotel in the main street. The cathedral is a short walk away, the Viking ships a longer walk through a lovely park. Comfortable, with good facilities.
First Resort Mogenstrup Kro, Præsto Landevej 25, Mogenstrup, 4700 Næstved, tel: 55 761130, fax: 55 761129. Very pretty hotel southeast of the town centre. Excellent base for touring. Very comfortable.

MID-RANGE

Hotel Hamlet, Bramstræde 5, 3000 Helsingør, tel: 49 210591, fax: 49 260130. Irresistable name, near centre (a good walk from Kronborg). Very pleasant and friendly.
Hotel Hillerød, Milnersvej 41, 3400 Hillerød, tel: 48 240800, fax: 48 240874. South of the town (and so a long walk from the castle) but delightful. Modern rooms, good facilities.

BUDGET

Danhostel Nykøbing Falster, Østre Allé 110, 4800 Nykøbing Falster, tel: 54 856699, fax: 54 823242. One of a chain of hostels across Denmark which offer dormitory and budget single/double room accommodation. Basic, but friendly and clean. Ideally sited for exploring Lolland, Falster and Møn.

WHERE TO EAT

The Zealand towns have to compete with Copenhagen and have some fine restaurants, with both Danish and international cuisine. One that deserves a special mention is:

Stigann, Skt Getrudsstræde 2, 4600 Køge, tel: 56 630330, fax: 56 630342.

SHOPPING

Nothing really to compete with Copenhagen's shopping, but the larger towns have good centres. One of the best is the Stor-Center at Næstved – the largest shopping centre on Zealand outside the capital.

TOURS AND EXCURSIONS

Tourist Information Offices have details of tours and excursions. Most of Zealand's major sites can be reached on excursions from Copenhagen.

USEFUL CONTACTS

Tourist Information Offices:
Havnepladsen 3, 3000 Helsingør, tel: 49 211333, fax: 49 211577;
Slangerupgade 2, 3400 Hillerød, tel: 48 242626, fax: 48 242665;
Vestergade 1, 4600 Køge, tel: 56 676001, fax: 56 655984;
Det Gule Pakhus, Havnen 1, 4700 Næstved, tel: 55 721122, fax: 55 721667;
Østergågade 7, 4800 Nykøbing Falster, tel: 54 851303, fax: 54 851005;
Gullandsstræde 15, Postboks 637, 4000 Roskilde, tel: 46 316565, fax: 46 316560;
Storegade 15, 4180 Sorø, tel: 57 821012, fax: 57 821013.

COPENHAGEN	J	F	M	A	M	J	J	A	S	O	N	D
AVERAGE TEMP. °C	0	0	2	7	12	16	18	17	14	9	5	3
AVERAGE TEMP. °F	32	32	36	45	54	61	64	63	57	48	41	37
RAINFALL mm	49	39	32	38	40	47	71	66	62	59	48	49
RAINFALL in	1.9	1.5	1.3	1.5	1.6	1.9	2.8	2.6	2.4	2.3	1.9	1.9

7
Bornholm

Set way out in the Baltic Sea, far closer to Sweden than the rest of Denmark (and closer to Germany and Poland too), **Bornholm** is the most unlikely part of the Danish kingdom. It has been inhabited since prehistoric times, as the wealth of burial mounds and rock engravings show, but become Danish only when southern Sweden was part of Denmark. In the 17th century during the wars between Denmark and Sweden it was occupied by the Swedes, but the islanders rebelled, killing the Swedish governor and throwing his troops out.

Scenically, southern Bornholm is much like Jutland. The white sand beaches have often been claimed to be the best in Europe, with **Dueodde** usually topping the list of favourites. The north of the island is a complete contrast (both to the south and the rest of Denmark), its angular granite cliffs reminding visitors of Norway. **Hammeren** is the place to see the best of the granite scenery.

Though many travel to Bornholm because of its tranquil remoteness, the island is not lacking in interesting sights. The island's four **round churches** are historically and architecturally important and there are exciting craft and art galleries which complement the scenic delights.

Travel to Bornholm takes about eight hours by ferry from Copenhagen, though only 75 minutes from Ystad in southern Sweden. Much quicker, of course, is the service run by Maersk Air from Copenhagen. On the island, the bus service is useful for those not wanting to hire a car. A good alternative, bearing in mind the island is only 40km (25 miles) along its long axis, is hiring a bicycle.

DON'T MISS

*** Hammeren: fantastic rock architecture, Hammershus, a vast ruined fortress and a series of ancient rock carvings.
** Dueodde: a beach of amazingly white sand.
** Østerlars Church: the best of Bornholm's round churches.
* Bornholms Kunstmuseum: an interesting collection in an equally interesting building.

Opposite: *A colourful half-timbered house in Rønne's old town.*

THE LIBERATION OF BORNHOLM

Germany occupied Bornholm in World War II. In May 1945 the German commander, fearful of Soviet capture, offered to surrender to British troops, but then fired on a Soviet surveillance plane. A few hours later a Soviet bomber squadron bombed Rønne and Nexø, killing several locals. The Soviets then ordered the Germans to surrender and, when they didn't, bombed the island again. Now the Germans surrendered and Bornholm was occupied by Soviet troops. They remained 10 months, for no good reason, pulling out suddenly in March 1946 just when it seemed Bornholm might never be liberated.

RØNNE AND A TOUR OF BORNHOLM

All trips to Bornholm start from **Rønne**, since the town is not only the island's capital, but the ferry port and the site of the airport. About one third of Bornholm's population of 45,000 live in the town. A tour of Rønne's old quarter is best started from Store Torv, where markets are still held on Wednesday and Saturday mornings. Go up Store Torvegade, then second left into Laksegade to reach **Erichsens Gård**, an early 19th-century merchant's house that is now part of the Bornholm Museum (open mid-Apr to mid-Oct Mon–Fri 10:00–17:00, Sat 10:00–14:00; mid-Oct to mid-Apr Mon–Sat 13:00–16:00). The house is furnished in period style. At the end of Laksegade turn left along Storegade in which stand the **Kommandantgården** (Commander's House), built in 1846, and the early 19th-century **Amtmandsgården** (old Sheriff's House). Jens Kofoed, who led the rebellion that ousted the Swedes and returned Bornholm to the Danish crown in 1658, was born in a house on this site. Between the two houses, on the left, is Krystalgade in which stands **Hjorths Fabrik**, a working ceramics museum (May–Oct Mon–Fri 10:00–17:00; Sat 10:00–14:00; Nov–Apr Mon–Fri 10:00–17:00, Sat 10:00–13:00).

Continue down Storegade to Kirkepladsen where the town church stands. Bear left, then left again to return to Store Torvet. Now bear right across the square to Sankt Martens Gade and the main **Bornholms Museum** site. Here there is a collection of the particular form of grandfather clock made on the island, but the high-

lights are the *Guldgubber,* a collection of small beaten gold artefacts, believed to be 6th-century votive offerings (open Easter to Sep Mon–Sat 10:00–17:00; Oct to Easter Tue–Sat 13:00–17:00). Another interesting museum is the **Forsvarsmuseet** (Defence Museum) in the Kastellet, a 17th-century fortress south

of the town. This has a collection of weaponry, but also deals with the liberation of Bornholm after World War II.

Above: *The ruins of Hammershus, a 13th-century fortress – the most famous landmark on Bornholm, and one of the most picturesque.*

To the north of Rønne, then inland, is **Nyker**, where the first (and smallest) of Bornholm's four round churches is located. It was built in the 12th century – but with a 16th-century roof. As with the other churches, it was built as fortress (probably against attacks by Wends) as well as church. The other three churches are on three floors, the upper being entirely defensive. At Nyker the third floor was not completed.

Hasle, further up the west coast, has some pretty houses and a church with a rare 15th-century altar rail. There is also a smokehouse, in part a museum, but still selling the smoked herring for which Bornholm is famous. At the northern tip of the island is **Hammeren**. Here the **Hammershus**, perched at the edge of a 75m (245ft) cliff, is the ruined remains of Europe's biggest fortress, built in the 13th century. Also here, the **Madsebakke Helleristninger** are a series of Bronze-Age rock carvings depicting, it is believed, the sun and footprints, but also ancient boats. The granite scenery of Hammeren is also superb.

Sandvig and **Allinge** on the east side of Hammeren are seaside resorts, while inland, at **Olsker**, is another round church, more slender than the others. Further along the coast, close to another area of fine granite cliffs, is **Bornholms Kunstmuseum**, the island's art museum. Housed in a new building is a collection of work by island artists covering the period from the late 19th

---

CLIMATE

As might be expected from its position, Bornholm is cooler and drier than the rest of Denmark. It is also **windier**, westerly winds dominating in summer, while the easterlies in winter bring in cold air from Russia. In **spring**, the range of flowers supported by the island's acid soil is astonishing.

ØSTERLARS ROUND CHURCH

The church dates from the mid-12th century and as well as the distinctive base and conical roof has seven big buttresses. Inside there are good frescoes rescued from beneath centuries of whitewash. It is believed that here, as elsewhere, the roof was originally flat so the defenders could harass attackers, the distinctive conical roof being a later addition.

century (open Jun–Aug daily 10:00–17:00, Apr, May, Sep and Oct Tue–Sun 10:00–16:00). **Gudhjem**, further south, is a seaside village with a history museum and a glassworks where visitors can watch the process. At nearby **Melsted** there is a museum of agriculture, while inland, the **Bornholms Middelaldercenter** is a celebration of medieval island life with reconstructed buildings and craft workers (open May–Jun daily 10:00–16:00, Jul to mid-Aug 10:00–17:00, mid-Aug to Sep 10:00–16:00). Close by is the **Østerlars** round church.

At Bornholm's eastern tip is **Svaneke**, a charming little town with many craft workers, and Joboland, which children will enjoy for its water slides, buggy racing and more (open May to mid-Sep daily 11:00–17:00 and 10:00–19:00 in Jul). From Gudhjem, Allinge and Svaneke ferries cross to the little island of **Christiansø**, a preserved 17th-century fortress island and the most remote part of Denmark. To the south of Svaneke is **Nexø**, the island's second largest town, often used as a touring centre, particularly for the beautiful beach at **Dueodde**, the island's southern tip. Dueodde sand is so fine that it was once used in hourglasses.

Below: *The church at Østerlars, the best of the four round churches on Bornholm.*

Inland of Nexø there is some of Denmark's best woodland, which can be explored by a number of marked trails. At **Aakirkeby** there is a museum of old vehicles (open mid-Jun to Sep Mon–Fri 11:00–17:00), and there is also **Natur-Bornholm**, which explores the development of the island's natural history (open Apr–Oct daily 10:00–17:00). Finally, on the road from Aakirkeby to Rønne is **Nylars**, which is where you'll find the last of Bornholm's round churches.

Bornholm at a Glance

Come to this part of the country in spring for the flowers, in summer for the glorious beaches and cliff walks, in autumn for the sunsets over the Baltic, and in winter if you want to have the place more or less to yourself.

There is an Airport at Rønne, with regular flights to and from Copenhagen. There are also ferries from Copenhagen. If you are touring Scandinavia, then a very good idea is to use the shorter ferry crossing from Ystad in southern Sweden and then to fly to Copenhagen after enjoying the island.

There is a reasonable bus service operated by BAT which links Rønne with all the main towns and villages. BAT also operates specific services which will be of interest to visitors. The Handicrafts Bus tours work-shops and studios, while the Veteran Bus tours old-fashioned work areas for those interested in the devel-opment of the island. The Garden Bus tours beautiful gardens, the Medieval Bus is for those interested in the island's historical sites, and the NaturBornholm Bus is for those more interested in wild Bornholm. Bicycle hire is also widely available and certainly worth considering.

There are good hotels on the island, mostly in or around Rønne. Worth considering are:

LUXURY

Radisson SAS Fredensborg Hotel, Strandvejen 116, 3700 Rønne, tel: 56 954444, fax: 56 950314. Beautifully sited on a wooded hill south of the capital. The best on the island.

MID-RANGE

Hotel Balka Søbad, Boule-varden 9, 3730 Nexø, tel: 56 492225, fax: 56 492233. At Balka, the beach area south of Nexø. Nicely sited for those looking for beach as well as touring. Good facilities.

BUDGET

Danhostel Gudhjem, Ejnar Mikkelsensvej 14, 3760 Gudhjem, tel: 56 485035, fax: 56 485635. Another of the Danhostel chain of budget hotels/hostels. Very good value and off the beaten track.

The island is famous for its herring and Baltic salmon based menus, and every town and village will offer the visitor a chance to try them

Shoppers expecting a vast range of possibilities will be a little disappointed, and also restricted to Rønne. But all over the island there are chances to buy island crafts – knitwear and ceramics in particular.

The Tourist Information Offices have details of sight-seeing tours and excursions. The BAT bus options are certainly worth considering.

Tourist Information Offices:
Torvet 2, 3720 Aakirkeby, tel: 56 974520, fax: 56 975890; Kirkegade 4, 3770 Allinge, tel: 56 480901, fax: 56 480020; Åbogade 9, 3760 Gudhjem, tel: 56 485210, fax: 56 485274; Kartemagergården, Havnegade 1, 3790 Hasle, tel: 56 964481, fax: 56 964106; Postboks 65, 3730 Nexø, tel: 56 497079, fax: 56 497010; Nordre Kystvej 3, 3700 Rønne, tel: 56 959500, fax: 56 959568; Stregade 24, 3740 Svaneke, tel: 56 497079, fax: 56 497010.

RØNNE	J	F	M	A	M	J	J	A	S	O	N	D
AVERAGE TEMP. °C	1	0	2	6	12	16	17	17	14	10	6	2
AVERAGE TEMP. °F	34	32	36	43	54	59	63	63	57	50	43	36
RAINFALL mm	35	25	20	27	30	35	50	51	50	44	43	38
RAINFALL in	1.4	1.0	0.8	1.1	1.2	1.4	2.0	2.0	2.0	1.7	1.7	1.5

Travel Tips

Tourist Information

Denmark has tourist offices in all European capitals, in North America, Australia, South Africa and Japan. In Denmark the main office is **Danish Tourist Board**, Vesterbrogade 6D, 1620 Copenhagen V, tel: 33 931416. There are tourist offices in all main towns and most large villages throughout the country. Most offices offer help with booking accommodation and will also assist with travel. The Wonderful Copenhagen office at Vestersrogade 1, tel: 70 222442 or 33 111325, is excellent for the city and the area around it, including the main sites on northeast Zealand.

Entry Requirements

A valid passport is required by all travellers. For visitors from European Union (EU) countries a national identity card will do. Visitors from most European countries, North America, Australia and New Zealand do not require visas. Visitors from Asia, Africa and most ex-Soviet bloc countries do require a visa. If in doubt, ask at your Danish Tourist Board office.

Customs

Visitors from countries outside the EU are restricted to one litre of spirits or two litres of fortified or sparking wine, together with two litres of table wine, and 200 cigarettes. Visitors from EU countries will know that 'duty free' items are no longer available when travelling between Union countries. However, there are still rules which apply to what may be brought into the country, duty-paid from another EU country – the limits are 1.5 litres of spirits or 20 litres of sparkling wine or 90 litres of table wine, and 300 cigarettes or 400g of tobacco. There is no limit on the amount of beer which can be imported from EU countries.

Health Requirements

Denmark has no specific health requirements for visitors. Visitors from countries with reciprocal agreements with Denmark are covered by the Danish national health programme. For visitors from EU countries this means you must carry an E111 form and present it when you seek treatment. However, such visitors need to be aware that there are advantages in also having travel insurance (for instance in getting home quickly and, if necessary, with medical assistance). All visitors to Denmark are entitled to free hospital attention in the event of accidents or sudden medical emergencies, provided that they did not travel to the country with the express purpose of receiving such treatment. Visitors from other countries should therefore check the validity and cover of their own medical insurance.

Getting There

By Air: Denmark is 'co-owner' of SAS (Scandinavian Airlines) together with Norway and Sweden, and SAS is the major carrier into the country. Other European and world airlines also operate flights to Copenhagen.
By Sea: DFDS Seaways operate services to Copenhagen from Oslo, (via Helsingborg in Sweden) and to Esbjerg from Harwich in the UK. Color Line

operate between several cities in Norway and Hirtshals, north Jutland. Stena Line operate ferries between Norway, Sweden and Denmark (principally Oslo, Gothenburg and Copenhagen). There are ferries between German ports and Denmark (Puttgarden to Rødbyhavn, Rostock to Gedser, Sylt to Rømø, Sassnitz to Bornholm. Ferries also reach Bornholm from Ystad and Kristianstad in Sweden. Polferries also operate services from Swinoujscie to Copenhagen and Bornholm. Smyril Line operate a service which links Hanstholm with the Faroe Islands and Iceland.

By Train: Denmark is connected by rail to all major cities in Europe, and beyond.

By Road: The E45 motorway crosses Denmark's only land border with another European country (Germany) and can be used as an access point for all European countries. The new Øresund bridge now also offers a motorway connection to Sweden and, via its motorway system, to Norway and Finland.

What to Pack

There is nothing particularly hostile about the Danish climate. As a northern European country it is cooler than those around the Mediterranean, particularly in the winter when very cold temperatures can occur if the weather is coming from the east. In summer a raincoat/jacket is essential as you are likely to see rain. The sky is also likely to be overcast at times too, so something

warm will probably be useful. Denmark is highly civilized and so will have anything you can think of on sale, so there is no need to burden yourself with unnecessary items (though it is worth noting that the cost of living is high, so such things as film – which you will need a lot of as there are great things to photograph – will probably be more expensive).

Money Matters

Denmark has not, as yet, joined the Eurozone and so maintains its own currency, the **krone** (crown – plural **kroner**). The krone is divided into 100 øre, but there are only coins for 25 and 50 øre. There are 1, 2, 10 and 20 kroner coins and 50, 100, 200, 500 and 1000 kroner notes. The krone is a convertible currency and so can be purchased abroad. Most Danish banks have ATM machines for credit and bank cards. Traveller's cheques can be readily exchanged at all banks.

Accommodation

Denmark has a large number of excellent hotels, all towns and most large villages having something to offer the visitor. Several chains – Best Western, First, etc. – have numerous hotels throughout the country. Visitors intending to follow all or part of the Margueritruten (the Marguerite Route – see panel, page 27) should ask the local Tourist Office for a leaflet on the **Marguerit Hoteller**, a series of hotels of great character set along the route. Budget travellers should ask for

details of the Danhostel chain. These basic, but clean and friendly, hotels offer dormitory accommodation and, at a higher price, single and double rooms. They are dotted throughout the country and are usually conveniently sited for train and bus travellers. Denmark also has several youth hostels. It also has an excellent number of bed and breakfast places. These have the advantage not only of being inexpensive, but of allowing travellers to meet Danish people. There is a large number of camp sites, chiefly around the coast. The biggest concentration is on the western coast of Jutland where they attract German visitors. There are, though, sites in all areas. Many camp sites also offer cabins for rent. On Bornholm, many visitors chose to camp and use bicycles to get around, making

NATIONAL HOLIDAYS

1 January • New Year's Day (Nyårsdag)
March/April • Maundy Thursday (Skærtorsdag)
March/April • Good Friday (Langfredag)
March/April • Easter Monday (2.påskedag)
4th Friday after Easter • Day of Prayer (Stor Bededag)
6th Thursday after Easter • Ascension Day (Kristi Himmelfartsdag)
8th Monday after Easter • Whit Monday (2.pinsedag)
5 June • Constitution Day (Grundlovsdag)
24–26 December • Christmas (Jule)

the most of the island's relatively flat, but interesting country.

Eating Out

Eating out is one of the joys of a visit to Denmark as the menu will be packed with wholesome meals. Fish is a speciality, not only at coastal towns, some visitors coming across herrings in all their forms for the first time at breakfast needing a little time to adjust. Baltic salmon is another speciality. The larger towns will offer not only Danish cuisine, but restaurants selling Chinese (very popular), Indian, Japanese and other menus. Opposite one of the very best Danish restaurants in the country (in Odense) there is, as an interesting alternative, a Mongolian restaurant. All restaurants and cafés serve tea and coffee, and most also serve hot chocolate. The latter is usually extremely good, and especially warming on cold winter days. Carslberg and Tuborg beers and lagers are sold in most restaurants and bars. The Danes have a much more relaxed attitude to alcohol than their Scandinavian neighbours who believe that allowing citizens the right to buy alcohol more or less as they wish is the road to ruin. This does mean that visitors may come across Swedes who have crossed on the ferry from Helsingborg or Malmö whose consumption has been rather too enthusiastic, or be surprised by the quantities being bought by Swedes at shops. The Danes take all this in their stride – indeed, it is an oft

repeated tale that the dimensions of the boot of Volvo cars were worked out around the size of cases of Carlsberg.

Tipping

Service is usually included on restaurant and hotel bills, and even taxi fares, so check first. The 'standard' rate is 10%, but the Danes themselves are not the world's greatest tippers so the rule that the tip rewards very good service should apply.

Transport

Air: SAS has domestic services to Aalborg, Århus, Billund, Sønderborg, Odense and Bornholm. Maersk Air also runs some domestic services.
Trains: There is an excellent rail service (operated by DSB – Danske Stasbaner – Danish State Railways) across the country, linking Copenhagen with all major towns in a matter of a few hours.
Buses: There are excellent bus services from Copenhagen to the major towns in Jutland, Fyn and Zealand. At the more local level the service tends to be good, but infrequent.
Road: With the building of the bridges over the Great Belt and the Little Belt (though the latter was a new bridge for the motorway as there had been a bridge for many years) the road connections across the country are now excellent. Formerly road users had to wait for ferries which were sometimes disrupted by (and occasionally cancelled due to) bad weather. It is now possible to travel to Aalborg, Esbjerg, Aabrenaa,

Helsingør and Rødbyhavn from Copenhagen by motorway in just a few hours (or much less in the case of the last two places). The Great Belt Bridge is a toll bridge. The toll booths accept both cash and credit cards. The bridge over the Øresund has also linked Copenhagen and Malmö, a journey which also formerly required a ferry crossing (occasionally in weather that sorted out the sailors from the non-sailors). The Øresund crossing is also a toll bridge. Cash in Danish or Swedish krone, or credit cards can be used. Neither the Great Belt nor the Øresund bridges are cheap, but when compared to the time saving and the expense of their construction they cannot really be considered expensive.
Cars: Denmark drives on the right. Seat belts are compulsory for all occupants. Children under three years of age must be secured in a child seat or approved restraint. Motor cyclists must wear crash helmets. Fines for speeding and other traffic offences (e.g. failing to stop at a halt sign,

ROAD SIGNS
Ensrettet • One-way Street
Fodgængere • Pedestrians
Jernbaneoversæring • Level Crossing
Parkering Forbudt • No Parking
Rundkørsel • Roundabout
Skole • School
Vejarbejde • Road Works
Overhaling Forbudt • No Overtaking

not wearing a seat belt) can be collected on the spot. They are expensive and non-negotiable. There is an on-the-spot fine for using a mobile telephone while driving. The speed limits are: 50kph (30mph) in towns and built-up areas; 80kph (50mph) on major roads; 110kph (70mph) on motorways. The blood alcohol limit is 0.05%. It is rigorously imposed and the penalties are non-trivial, with hefty fines and prison sentences.

Bicycles: For local exploration, even in the cities, bicycles are a good idea. Denmark has cycle lanes on almost all its roads and also in towns and cities, and drivers actually take note of them.

Business Hours

Shops are usually open from 09:30–17:30 weekdays and 09:30–14:00 on Saturdays. However, in most towns with large numbers of visitors, and those geared particularly to tourist trade, the closing time is often much later. In Copenhagen's Strøget for instance, even in winter it is unusual to find shops closing before 19:00, and often much later. Businesses usually open 09:00–16:00 Monday–Friday, with banks opening 10:00–16:00 weekdays (but until 18:00 on Thursdays).

Time Difference

Denmark operates on Central European Time which is one hour ahead of Greenwich Mean Time (GMT). Daylight saving sees the clocks move one hour forward on the last Sunday in March and one hour back on the last Sunday in October. When it is 12:00 in Denmark it is 11:00 in London, 01:00 in Washington DC, 03:00 in San Francisco, 23:00 in Auckland, 21:00 in Sydney, 19:00 in Perth and 13:00 in Cape Town.

Communications

There are post offices in all towns and large villages. They normally keep shop hours. Most towns have public telephones – particularly at train and bus stations. These usually take phonecards – available at post offices, kiosks and some

USEFUL PHRASES

Yes/No • Ja/Nej
Please • Vær venlig
Thank you • Tak
Good morning • Godmorgen
Good evening • Godaften
Excuse me • Undskyld
Where is ... ? • Hvor er ... ?
How much? • Hvor meget?
How many? • Hvor mange?
When? • Hvornår?
What? • Hvad?
Who? • Hvem?
Why? • Hvorfor?
Which? • Hvilken?
What does this mean? • Hvad betyder dette?
Can you help me? • Kan De hjælpe mig?
I am lost • Jeg har gået vild
I don't understand • Jeg forstår ikke
My name is ... • Jeg hedder ...
Help • Hjælp
Go away • Forsvind
Call the doctor/police/ ambulance • Ring efter en læge/politiet/en ambulance
Toilets • Toiletter
Men/Women • Herre/Damer
train • toget
bus • bussen (city) or rutebilen (long distance)
boat • båden
open • åben
closed • lukket
entrance • indgang
exit • udgang
forbidden • forbudt

CONVERSION CHART

FROM	TO	MULTIPLY BY
Millimetres	Inches	0.0394
Metres	Yards	1.0936
Metres	Feet	3.281
Kilometres	Miles	0.6214
Square kilometres	Square miles	0.386
Hectares	Acres	2.471
Litres	Pints	1.760
Kilograms	Pounds	2.205
Tonnes	Tons	0.984

To convert Celsius to Fahrenheit: x 9 ÷ 5 + 32

newsagents – or cash. The code for international calls is 00, followed by the country code. The country code for Denmark is 45. Faxes can be sent from most larger post offices. As would be expected for so go-ahead a country, there are facilities for using the internet in most towns.

Electricity

Denmark has a 50Hz, 220V AC electricity system utilizing the standard continental two-pin plug. UK visitors will need a three-pin to two-pin adapter. Visitors from North America with 110V/115V appliances will need a transformer to make them work.

Weights and Measures

Denmark uses the metric system of weights and measures, that is the kilogram, metre, litre system. On the roads distance are measured in kilometres and speed limits are given in kph.

Health Precautions

Denmark is a healthy place where it is safe to drink the water and the chances of having stomach upsets or catching curious illnesses is minimal.

Health Services

The Danish health system is one of the best in Europe with well-staffed and equipped hospitals and well-qualified doctors and dentists. As noted above, EU visitors should carry their EHIC card. All visitors should understand the terms and conditions of their medical insurance.

Personal Safety

Denmark is as safe as any European country. This means that the usual rules of safety should be applied – do not leave valuables on display in parked cars, use safety deposit boxes in hotels and be careful in crowded city areas or when travelling at night. As with all developed countries Denmark has a drug problem and this brings petty crime in its wake. The rules of safety you apply in your own country should see you safely through your visit.

Emergencies

For ambulance, fire service and police telephone 112.

Etiquette

Danes are friendly and helpful and the normal rules of a polite, civilized society apply (though they do not queue well, most queues breaking down into a free-for-all when the bus, train, etc. arrives). As always, knowing the Danish words for 'please' and 'thank you' is appreciated.

Language

Danish is a Scandinavian language derived form the original Viking language, itself a Germanic tongue. Danes, Norwegians and Swedes can talk to each other in their own languages and be understood, differences being similar to dialects in other languages. By contrast, Icelanders who talk a language virtually identical to the Viking tongue can neither understand or be understood. Most Danes speak very good English – I was memorably accosted by a drunk early one morning in Copenhagen and, trying the 'no understand' ploy to get away told him I was English. He apologized and repeated his question (do you have the time please) in perfect English.

Danish has all the letters of the English alphabet plus three more – æ, ø and å (the capitals are Æ, Ø and Å)

Festivals

Denmark has a whole host of festivals throughout the year, some international (music, arts, film, etc.), some more local, perhaps based on a local legend. It is worth finding out if there is anything coming up from the local Tourist Office as Danes know how to have a good time.

GOOD READING

- **Dyrbye, Helen; Harris, Steven;** and **Golzen, Thomas** (1999) *Xenophobe's Guide to the Danes* (Oval)
- **Graham-Campbell, James** (1980) *The Viking World* (Ticknor and Fields)
- **Høeg, Peter** (1996) *Miss Smilla's Feeling for Snow* (The Harvill Press)
- **Hornshoj-Møller, Stig** (1998) *A Short History of Denmark* (Grafisk)
- **Strathern, Paul** (1997) *Kierkegaard in 90 Minutes* (Ivan R Dee Publisher)
- **Thomas, Alistair H** and **Oakley, Stewart P** (1998) *Historical Dictionary of Denmark* (The Scarecrow Press)
- **Andersen, Hans Christian** (1993) *The Complete Fairy Tales* (Gramercy Books)

INDEX

Note: Numbers in **bold**
indicate photographs

Aabenraa 84
Aakirkeby 120
Aalborg 62–64
accommodation 58, 75,
  85, 97, 115, 121, 123
Ærø 95
akvavit 29, 62
Ålestrup 66
Als Island 8, 84
Anderson, Hans Christian
  4, 5, 27, 34, 50, 87, 90
Århus 70–72
Arken Art Gallery 99, **110**
Arkitekcentret,
  Christianshavn 54
Assens 92

Bishop Absalon 31, 39, 42
Black Diamond,
  Copenhagen **27**, 44
Blixen, Karen 27
Bluetooth, Harald 68, 102
Bogense 92
Bon Bon Land, Holme-
  Østrup 112
Børglum, Fårup 65
Bornholm 9, 117–120
Bornholms Middelalder-
  center 120
Brahe, Tycho 42, 56
Brandts Klædefabrik, Fyn
  91
Bulbjerg 66
Bundgaard, Anders 50

Carlsberg Brewery,
  Copenhagen **57**
Carstensen, Georg 36, 37
castles and palaces
  Aalborghus Slot,
    Aalborg 63
  Amalienborg Slot,
    Frederiksstaden 47
  Charlottenborg,
    Nyhavn 46
  Christiansborg Slot,
    Slotsholmen **42**
  Egeskov, South Fyn **94**
  Fredensborg Slot,
    Northeast Zealand
    107
  Frederiksberg Slot,
    Vesterbro 57
  Frederiksborg Slot,
    Hillerød 106, **108**
  Kronborg Castle,
    Helsingør **107**
  Levetzau Palace,
    Frederiksstaden 47
  Nyborg 95

castles and palaces (cont.)
  Rosenborg Slot **21**, 53
  Selsø Castle, Northeast
    Zealand 105
  Valdemars Slot, Tåsinge
    95
Christiania **23**, 55
Christiansen, Ole Kirk 79
Christianshavn Kanal 55
Christiansø Island 120
churches and cathedrals
  Alexander Newsky
    Kirke,Frederiksstaden
    48
  Cathedral of St Knud,
    Odense **86**, 89
  Christianskirke,
    Christianshavn 54
  Domkirke, Århus 71
  Elmelunde Church,
    Møn 114
  Frederikskirken,
    Frederiksstaden **47**
  Helligåndskirken,
    Strøget 39
  Højerup Church **111**
  Holmenskirken,
    Slotsholmen 43
  Marmorkirken see
    Frederikskirken
  Rømø Kirke, South
    Jutland **83**
  Sankt Albani Kirke,
    Odense 89
  Sankt Ansgar Kirke,
    Frederiksstaden 49
  Sankt Bendts Kirke,
    Ringsted 111
  Sankt Martens Kirke,
    Randers 68
  Sankt Nicolai Kirke,
    Vejle 78
  Sankt Nikolaj Kirke,
    Strøget 40
  Sankt Pauls Kirke,
    Frederiksstaden 50
  Slotskirke, Slotsholmen
    43
  St Albans Kirke,
    Frederiksstaden 50
  Vor Frelsers Kirke,
    Christianshavn **55**
  Vor Frue Kirke, Aalborg
    63
  Vor Frue Kirke, Århus 71
  Vor Frue Kirke, Strøget
    39
Commoner's Tower, Ribe
  77
Copenhagen **20**, 30–59
CW Obels Plads, Aalborg
  62, **63**

Dannebrog **24**
Den Gamle Kro (The Old
  Inn), Odense **91**

Den Kongelige Afstøbnings-
  samlingen 47
Den Lille Havfrue 50, **51**
Det Gyldne Tårn,
  Copenhagen 37
Djursland 9, 72
dolmen **12**
Dream Castle, Aalborg **66**
Dueodde 117, 120

Ebeltoft 72
economy 24–25
emergencies 126
Eriksen, Edvard 50
Esbjerg 80–81

Faaborg 93
Falster Island 8, 99, 113
Fantasy World, Ringsted
  112
flag see Dannebrog
flora and fauna 10, **11**, 12
food and drink 28–29, 59,
  75, 85, 97, 115, 121,
  124
fountains, Copenhagen
  Bubble Fountain 37
  Caritas Fountain **38**, 39
  Dragon's Leap Fountain
    34
  Gefion Fountain **50**
  Storkespringvandet 40
Fredericia 78
Frederikshavn 64
Frederiksholms Kanal **41**
Frederikssund 104
Frederiksværk 105
Fyn 31, 87–97
Fyrkat 68

Gilleleje 106
Givskud 78
Gjern 74
Golden Crown **53**
Golden Tower see Det
  Gyldne Tårn
government 24
Gram 84
Grauballe Man 72
Great Belt Bridge **102**
Grenaa 72
Grubbe Mølle, Fyn 93
Gudenå River 6, 68
Gudhjem 120

Haderslev 84
Hammeren 117
Hammershus **119**
Hanstholm 66
Hasle 119
HC Andersens Hus,
  Odense 90
health 122
Helsingør 99, **106**
Herning 69
Himmelbjerg 74

Himmerland 67
Hirtshals 64, **65**
history 12–24
Hjørring 65
Hobro 68
Højer 7, 84
Højerup 8, 111
Holbæk 101
Holme-Østrup 112
Holmsland Klit 7, 70
Hornbæk 8, 106
Horne 93
Horsens 78
Humlebæk 8
Hundested 106
Hvide Sande 70

Jacobsen, Carl 38, 50
Jægerspris 105
Jelling **18**, 61, 77
Jutland 5, **6**, 7, 61–85

Kalundborg 100
Kerteminde 96
Klitmøller 66
Knud the Holy **19**
Køge 110
Kolding 78
Kong Humbles Grav,
  Langeland 95
Kongens Nytorv,
  Copenhagen **44**, 45
Korsør 100
Krudttårnet (Gunpowder
  Tower), Frederikshavn
  64
Kvistgård 107

Ladby 96
Langeland Island 95
Legoland 61, 77, 79, **80**
Lemvig 65
Lille Mølle (Little
  Windmill),
  Christianshavn 55
Lillebælt (Little Belt) 87
Limfjorden 62, 65–66
Lindholm Høje **64**
Lintrup 81
Little Heddinge Windmill
  98
Little Mermaid see Den
  Lille Havfrue
Løgumkloster 84
Lolland Island 8, **113**
Louisiana Art Gallery,
  Humlebæk 99, **109**

Madsebakke
  Helleristninger,
  Hammeren 119
Maren Turis Gade, Aalborg
  60
Mariager 68
Marmorbræn, Copenhagen
  42

Melsted 120
merchant houses
  Den Smidtske Gård,
    Vejle 78
  Erichsens Gård, Rønne
    118
  Jens Bangs Stenhus,
    Aalborg 63
  Jorgen Olufsens Gård,
    Aalborg 63
Middelaldercentret,
  Lolland 113
Middelfart 91, 92
Mogeltonder 83
Møn Island 99, **114**
Monastery of the Holy
  Ghost, Aalborg 62
Møns Klint 8, **114**
museums
  Anne Hvides Gård,
    Svendborg 94
  Arbejdermuseet,
    Rosenborg 53
  Art Museum, Horsens
    78
  Bakkehusmuseet,
    Vesterbro 57
  Bangsbomuseet,
    Frederikshavn 64
  Bornholm Museum 118
  Bornholms
    Kunstmuseum 119
  Botanical Museum,
    Rosenborg 52
  Burmeister & Wien
    Museet,
    Christianshavn 54
  Bymuseum,
    Frederiksværk 106
  Circus Museum, Rold 68
  Danish Maritime
    Museum, Helsingør
    107
  Den Fynske Landsby,
    Odense 91
  Den Gamle By, Århus
    72
  Den Hirschsprungske
    Samling, Rosenborg
    52
  Denmark's National
    Photographic Museum
    Herning 70
  Forsvarsmuseet,
    Bornholm 119
  Frihedsmuseet,
    Frederiksstaden 50
  Frilandsmuseum,
    Lolland 113
  Fyns Kunstmuseum,
    Fyn 91
  Geology Museum,
    Rosenborg 52
  Glasmuseet, Ebeltoft 72
  Guinness World Records
    Museum, Strøget 41

museums (cont.)
  Historical Museum,
    Aalborg 63
  History Museum,
    Herning 70
  Hjorths Fabrik, Rønne
    118
  Hollufgård, Odense 91
  Høve Museum, West
    Zealand 102
  Jernbanemuseum,
    Odense 91
  JF Williamsens Museum,
    Frederikssund 104
  Jysk Motor Museum,
    Gjern 74
  Karen Blixen Museum,
    Rungsted 113
  Københavns Bymuseet,
    Vesterbro 56
  Kunstindustrimuseet,
    Frederiksstaden 49
  Kvindemuseet, Århus 71
  Lilleskov Teglværk,
    West Fyn 92
  Louis Tussaud's Wax
    Museum,
    Copenhagen 35
  Mads Lerches Gåde,
    Nyborg 96
  Moesgård Museum,
    Århus 71
  Møntergården, Odense
    90
  Motor and Aircraft
    Museum, South Fyn
    95
  Museum Erotica,
    Strøget 40
  Museum of Medical
    History,
    Frederiksstaden 49
  Museum of Potatoes,
    Otterup 92
  Musical History
    Museum, Rosenborg
    53
  National Photographic
    Museum, Slotsholmen
    44
  Nationalmuseet,
    Slotsholmen **40**, 41
  Natural History
    Museum, Skagen 64
  Nordjyllands Kunst-
    museum, Aalborg 63
  Nyboders Mindestuer,
    Frederiksstaden 50
  Orlogsmuseet,
    Christianshavn 55
  Post and
    Telecommunications
    Museum, Strøget 40
  Roskilde Museum 104
  Silkeborg Kuntsmuseum
    74

museums (cont.)
  Silkeborg Museum 73
  Skitsesamling, Køge 110
  Statens Museum for
    Kunst, Rosenborg 52
  Thorvaldsens Museum,
    Slotsholmen 43
  Tobacco Museum,
    Strøget 39
  Tøjhusmuseet,
    Slotsholmen 43
  Town Museum, Faaborg
    93
  Town Museum,
    Middelfart 91
  Toy Museum, Køge 111
  Vikingemuseet, Århus 71
  Zeppelin Museum,
    Tønder 83

NaturBornholm, Aakirkeby
  120
Næstved 112
Nexø 120
Nyborg 87, 95–**96**
Nykøbing Falster 113

Odense 88–91
Øm Monastery, Ry 74
Østerlars **120**
Overby 102

parks
  Bakken Park,
    Klampenborg 109
  Frederiksberg Have,
    Vesterbro 57
  Jesperhus, Mors 65
  Knuthenborg Safari
    Park, Lolland 113
  Kongens Have,
    Rosenborg **52**, 53
  Tivoli, Århus 72
  Tivoli, Copenhagen
    35–38
people 25–29

Queen Margrethe's tomb
  103

Råbjerg Mile 7, 64
Randers 68
Rasmussen, Knud **105**
Rebild Bakker National
  Park 9, 67
Reersø 100
restaurants see food and
  drinks
Ribe **17**, 61, 77, 81–**82**
Ringkøbing 70
Ringsted 111
Ripley's Believe It or Not!
  35
Rold 68
Rold Skov 9, 67
Rømø 7, 82

Romsø 96
Rønne **116**, 118
Roskilde 99, 102–104
round churches
  Bornholm 117, 119,
    120
  Horne, Fyn **93**
Royal Cast Collection see
  Den Kongelige
  Afstøbningssamlingen
Royal Copenhagen
  Porcelain Factory 57
Rundetårn (Round Tower),
  Copenhagen 40
Rungsted 99, 108
Ry 74

shopping 59, 75, 85, 97,
  115, 121
Silkeborg 9, 61, 73–74
Skælskør 100
Skærbæk 83
Skagen 7, 64
Skive 65
Skuldelev 105
Slagelse 100
Slangerup 104
Sommerland, Varde 81
Sonderberg 84
Sorø 100
St Mary's Tower, Ribe **76**
Storebælt 87
Struer 65
Stubbekøbing 114
Sun Chariot **14**
Svaneke 120
Svendborg 94

Tåsinge 95
Thisted 66
Tisvildeleje 106
Tivoli, Copenhagen **36**, **37**
Tollund Man **73**
Tønder 83
tourist information 122
tours and excursions 59,
  75, 85, 97, 115, 121
Tranekær 95
transport 58, 75, 85, 97,
  115, 121, 124
Trelleborg **16**, 100
Trundholm Moor 101

useful contacts 59, 75, 85,
  97, 115, 121

Vejle 78
Vesterviig 66
Viborg 69
Viking ships **104**
Vikings 15, 16, 82, 100

windmills 74, **98**, 101

Zealand 99–114
Zoo, Copenhagen 57